Birthing the
SERMON

Birthing the SERMON

WOMEN PREACHERS *on the* CREATIVE PROCESS

Jana Childers, EDITOR

Chalice Press®
St. Louis, Missouri

Bible quotations, unless otherwise noted, are from the *New Revised Standard Version Bible,* copyright 1989, Division of Christian Education of the National Council of the Churches of Christ in the United States of America. Used by permission. All rights reserved.

Biblical quotations marked (JPS) are taken from *The TANAKH, the new JPS translation according to the taditional Hebrew text,* copyright © 1985 by the Jewish Publication Society. All rights reserved. Used by permission.

The photographs on pages 147 and 149 are the work of Dusty Stokes and were taken at Montclair Presbyterian Church.

The following materials in this book are used by permission:

Linda Clader, "Homily for the Feast of the Visitation." From *Preaching through the Year of Luke: Sermons That Work IX,* ed. by Roger Alling and David J. Schlafer, Morehouse Publishing.

Mary Oliver, "For poems are not words, after all." From *A Poetry Handbook* by Mary Oliver, Harcourt Brace and Co., Publishers.

Marge Piercy, "To be of use." From *Circles on the Water* by Marge Piercy, copyright © 1982 by Marge Piercy. Used by permission of Alfred A. Knopf, a division of Random House, Inc.

Barbara Brown Taylor, "Bothering God." Copyright 1999, Barbara Brown Taylor. All rights reserved. Reprinted from *Home By Another Way* by Barbara Brown Taylor; published by Cowley Publications, 28 Temple Place, Boston, MA 02111. www.cowley.org (1-800-225-1534).

Cover photograph: © D. Jeanene Tiner
Cover and interior design: Elizabeth Wright
Art direction: Elizabeth Wright

This book is printed on acid-free, recycled paper.

Visit Chalice Press on the World Wide Web at
www.chalicepress.com

10 9 8 7 6 5 4 3 2 1   01 02 03 04 05

Library of Congress Cataloging–in–Publication Data

Birthing the sermon : women preachers on creative process / edited by Jana Childers.
     p.   cm.
Includes bibliographical references.
ISBN 0-8272-0230-X
1. Preaching   2. Women clergy.   I. Childers, Jana.   II. Title.
BV4211.3   .B57   2001
251' .0082—dc21   00–011839

Printed in the United States of America

In Memory Of
Lucy Atkinson Rose

CONTENTS

INTRODUCTION

Preaching is a mother who conceives and gives birth to faith. It's a surprising metaphor. Preaching and mothers were not exactly love-and-marriage, horse-and-carriage words in the sixteenth century, nor in most of the centuries before and since. Even now when half the students going to mainline seminaries are women, there are those who wonder about the pairing. "What do mothers know about preaching?" "Do women have anything new to say about preaching?" "Is God really calling women to preach?" This book is an attempt to answer some of those questions.

As surprising as it may be, this is hardly a new metaphor. Even John Calvin, in a sermon on 1 Timothy 4:6–7, compared preachers with wet nurses. The dissolute nurse wastes her energies and has no milk to give the child, he wrote. But "she who will work readily, and will take food and sustenance along with her normal rest, she will be able also to feed her baby. So it is with those who have to preach the word of God."[1]

The twelve women whose work makes up this volume have something to say about conception and gestation, labor and delivery, nursing and feeding. Not all of us have been pregnant. Not all of us have raised children. Not all of us use the term *mother* to describe ourselves. But all of us know what all preachers, male and female, know. We know what it is like to conceive, nourish, and give birth to a sermon. Many of us also know what it is like to wonder about other people's processes. In the early days of our preaching ministries we remember worrying over whether we were doing it right. Was what we were doing in our studies on Tuesday mornings like what other women preachers were doing, like what the men who taught us were doing, or like some odd amalgam of the two? This book is an attempt to answer some of those questions too.

The contributors to this volume represent a wide spectrum of homiletical styles, theological traditions, and racial-ethnic communities. All of us are women who preach—but it is hard to find a single other thing the twelve of us have in common. Half of us are in parish ministry, half in teaching. We represent seven denominations and two major faith traditions. Some of us were born into the denominations in which we now minister; some of us have traveled across the theological spectrum to get to where we are. We are from the South, North, East, and West. Some of us agonize over the preparation process, and some of us find it to be pure joy. In terms of personality (at least according to the Myers-Briggs test), some of us are J's and some are P's. Some start preparing Sunday evening and work two and three-quarter hours each day; others write feverishly through Saturday night into the wee small hours of Sunday morning. Black and white, lesbian and straight, married and single, mother and not—we represent many, although not nearly all, of the demographic categories from which God is calling preachers.

The fact that we are women—people who have a certain experience with wombs, blood, cycles, menstrual pain, bloating, fatigue, anxiety, and the societal expectations that surround them— may not turn out to be the most important or interesting thing about this book. After all, some of the greatest creators (and creativity theorists) are men. On the other hand, where better to start a conversation about preachers' creative process than with the segment of the population who live in bodies that remind them constantly of creativity's rhythms? Who can comment more appropriately about changes in contemporary preaching than the newcomers who are causing (some of) them? What better encouragement is there for young preachers than the testimonies of those who have had to struggle to claim their place?

If John Calvin were alive today, I like to think he would take an interest in the question of preaching's "mothers." We know he liked the metaphor. Perhaps he would be willing to extend it. If preaching gives birth to faith, who gives birth to preaching, and how? How can a preacher find herself with enough milk to feed her baby? More than anything else, this book is an attempt to answer those questions.

Jana Childers
San Anselmo, California
Summer, 2000

CONTRIBUTORS

Barbara Shires Blaisdell is pastor of First Christian Church (Disciples of Christ) in Concord, California.

Teresa L. Fry Brown is assistant professor of homiletics at Candler School of Theology, Emory University, in Atlanta, Georgia, and a minister in the African Methodist Episcopal Church.

Jana Childers is professor of homiletics and speech-communication at San Francisco Theological Seminary in San Anselmo, California, and a minister in the Presbyterian Church (USA).

Linda L. Clader is professor of homiletics at Church Divinity School of the Pacific in Berkeley, California, and a priest in the Episcopal Church.

Yvette Flunder is pastor of City of Refuge in San Francisco, California, a congregation of the United Church of Christ.

Mary G. Graves is pastor of Trinity Presbyterian Church in San Carlos, California.

Linda Carolyn Loving is pastor of the House of Hope Presbyterian Church in St. Paul, Minnesota.

Barbara K. Lundblad is associate professor of preaching at Union Theological Seminary in New York City, New York, and a minister in the Evangelical Lutheran Church of America.

Karen Stokes is pastor of Montclair Presbyterian Church in Oakland, California.

Barbara Brown Taylor is the Harry R. Butman professor of Religion and Philosophy at Piedmont College in Demorest, Georgia, and a priest in the Episcopal Church.

Mary Donovan Turner is Carl Patton Associate Professor of Preaching at Pacific School of Religion in Berkeley, California, and a minister in the Christian Church (Disciples of Christ).

Margaret Moers Wenig is rabbi of Beth Am, The People's Temple, in New York City, New York, and instructor in liturgy and homiletics at Hebrew Union College, New York, New York.

CHAPTER 1

Barbara Shires
Blaisdell

I never intended to preach. I entered seminary not to pursue professional ministry but in search of something. Exactly what I was searching for was not at all clear to me. I was on my way to law school, to a profession that I hoped would help me make a real difference in a suffering world. The Christian faith of my childhood had lost credibility, given the suffering I had seen. The church of my childhood fell far short of its calling—that seemed all too clear to me. That my observations and my doubts about my faith and my church were not at all original did not occur to me. I entered seminary with questions, with outrage over the world's evil. I entered seminary with very few role models of women preachers and with ecclesial authorities relieved that I was "just" on a spiritual search and not on a career path toward ordination. I entered seminary to challenge the good people there and found instead that they shared my questions, my doubt, my righteous indignation at suffering and counted that as

1

faith. They taught me to notice the way in which my questions, doubt, and indignation at injustice were shared by God. They held out a vision of the church as a sign, an imperfect sign, to be sure, but a sign nevertheless, to the broken world of God's work toward healing and justice for the world. I left the seminary more assured but not completely certain about the faith. I left with hope but also with a lot of questions still about the church. I left, still not intending to preach. Twenty years later, after a lot of prompting and cajoling by God and the church, I enter a pulpit twice every week, week after week with fear and trembling, with belief shaded by doubt, with good news unavoidably shaped and nuanced by my own flawed soul.

I am very privileged to spend some of my time with young seminarians, both men and women. I find, especially in the women, a startling contrast to my own experience. They are far more certain of their call to ministry, far less haunted by self-doubt or even by doubts about the church. I am thrilled to know that they have experienced far fewer barriers on their paths to ordained ministry. But I am occasionally troubled by what appears to me sometimes as a sense of entitlement and ease about what Barbara Brown Taylor calls "the preaching life." And I wonder about my self-conscious struggle to write, week after week, a word of grace to a broken world from a broken heart. I wonder if that experience has anything to offer to my younger sisters just starting out in ministry. I am fairly sure, though, that five or ten years into ministry, after the first failures, after profound disillusionment with the church's petty power struggles, after the glorious joy of baptizing or dedicating babies and the depth of despair of burying friends in one's beloved congregation, the weekly experience of trying to find a word of grace for oneself and one's congregation has some common struggle. To that struggle, I will dare to speak a word about my experience in the hope that it may help another.

Inspiration and Routine

Foremost in that struggle: How do I find the time to write, to pray, to do adequate research? I am sure that God can be trusted to inspire a good word, week after week (even as I am restless with anxiety about just that each week). I am equally sure that God finds my heart and mind more open to that inspiration if both heart and mind are prepared and fertilized by prayer and study. Not that there haven't been times when I got into the pulpit totally unprepared, only to preach a sermon that seemed to move people and to offer them something of what they needed. But when I have let that experience make me lazy, my own soul goes hungry, and I cannot help but worry that the congregation is hungry as well.

So how do I find the time, amid the hospital calls and new member meetings, while writing liturgy and reports to the board, while supervising staff or trying to get a bulletin printed on ancient, inefficient equipment? It helps to break it up into manageable segments—and not to save it all for Saturday night. To be practical for a moment, I break up my study and preparation in this way.

On Monday I read the scripture, meditate, and journal. I use a form for meditation known as *Lectio Divina*. At this point, I am reading the scripture for my own soul. I am reading less for edification than for what my grandmother would have called sanctification. What is going on inside me? What does this sacred text have to say to me about that? How is the Spirit lifting me beyond myself in this text? On Monday, my task is to begin to glimpse and to pray over what in my life will enhance and what will hinder the gospel I am called to bring to the people the following Sunday.

On Tuesday I begin in the same way I did on Monday. I read the scripture. I pray and I journal. I also read commentaries on the text. These help open me up to aspects of the text that my own eyes did not see, to questions that I did not notice needed to be asked. The commentaries are the beginning of conversation with the Christian community and tradition. They often lead me to read more about history and cultural context. Sometimes they confirm the nudging I felt on Monday toward a particular direction for the sermon. Sometimes they seem to indicate that an honest appropriation of my own issues will provide manna for the following Sunday (whether or not I actually make personal reference to those issues—and I usually do not). Sometimes the commentaries reveal to me that my own issues are in the way of my seeing the gospel in the text. And the task becomes one of getting myself out of the way.

On Wednesday each week I reread the text, journal, and pray, looking back over what I have written two days before, looking forward a bit to where I might go. My Thursdays are set aside for writing a solid first draft. Thursdays are the hardest day of the week. I don't go into the office. I ask elders or colleagues to make all but life-and-death hospital calls. I have nothing to distract me but my own soul. Facing the blank computer screen every Thursday morning is an act of faith. I come to it filled with anxiety, and yet I sit down and begin to write in an attempt to live as if I trust my belief that God will indeed inspire a good word. Almost always words fall across the screen that I didn't know I knew, or believed, or understood, felicitous words for which I cannot take credit. I am sure that there are also words that are too narrowed by my own issues and agenda. But the experience of typing words that heal me, repeating them on a Sunday, and hearing that they had a healing effect on others convinces me that God does indeed provide a good and reliable word.

I have a generous congregation that allows me this whole day to pray and to write. I asked for it by quoting Urban Holmes, who in his book *Spirituality for Ministry* made a marvelous case for the importance of spiritual self-care for clergy and argued that parishioners would, on the whole, be comforted and not angered by being told that the minister was unavailable because he/she was praying and studying and writing.[1] There are those few parishioners who resent my Thursdays away from the office, but a very wise chair of my board of elders once said to me, "Letting those folks determine your priorities for ministry is like deliberately letting flies into your kitchen."[2]

Fridays are my day off. I play and rest and clean my house. My prayer life on Fridays is lighter and clearer and often provides a fun or funny insight into what I wrote the day before.

Saturdays, assuming Thursday went reasonably well, I spend two or three hours refining and rehearsing. There are Saturdays when I have to start all over, and the process takes all day. But I hate those, so I work really hard to have enough done by bedtime Thursday so that Saturday can be reasonably light.

Life Practices

In addition to a weekly routine, there are four life practices that aid my writing when I do them and hinder my work when I don't. I read constantly. I see a lot of movies. I get daily physical exercise. I write three pages of whatever junk is in my head and on my heart every morning as a prayer to God.

In order to keep my mind stimulated enough to produce eight to ten pages of creative material every week, I need to read constantly: theology and Biblical scholarship, of course. But I also find that good novels and writing that is honest about the human condition give me insight and perspective, even if I never use them in a sermon illustration. I don't read "sermon help" material. I don't find it helpful. But a reading of a novel like Anne Lamott's *Crooked Little Heart* is a winsome corrective for the current tendency (at least in Californian culture) to focus only on the "positive" side of human experience and human motivation.

In order to find time to read, I watch very little television. I am sure this puts me at a disadvantage in terms of the knowledge of pop culture. But the time it gives me is astounding. I do go to movies and rent movies and use them to make me more visual and more concrete in my preaching. I am hoping to be able to use video clips in worship within the next year, for I am convinced that the church must learn ways to better reach our culture of visual learners if we hope to communicate.

I also find that my writing improves when my body is active. I don't pretend to understand all the connections, but when I walk or hike or swim daily, I have more energy and perspective to write. Often, on my writing Thursday, I will get up early and write for several hours, only to be stuck by late morning. Then a long walk will do amazing things to clarify what it is I am trying to say, how it can better be ordered, and what is superfluous and can be ditched.

Finally, I try to write in prayer every morning three pages of whatever junk is in my head. This is rarely material for a sermon. This is material that gets in the way of a sermon. Because the writing is a form of prayer, it does lift whatever is on my heart to God. And getting it out on paper makes it less likely to get in the way of my other writing.

The sample sermon I am including here is one for Mother's Day in my congregation in Concord, California. Concord is about thirty miles east of San Francisco. It is a study in contrasts. It lies between San Francisco–Berkeley, one of the most diverse, liberal, postmodern places in the world, and California's great agricultural Central Valley, a place every bit as conservative as the midwest or new south. The congregation is pulled by that contrast. It is at once conservative and liberal, postmodern and fighting to hang on to many premodern and modern ideas and values. The challenge is to preach in a way that comforts the anxiety of living in a world of such rampant change and lack of cultural consensus about what is good and right and beautiful, while at the same time challenging the church's tendency to insularity and triumphalism. This particular sermon attempts to invite the listener to self-reflection about the limits of our ability to be in mission and ministry to the needy of the world if we do not recognize the needy within ourselves.

Mother to Mother: Centered in a Circle of Need

LUKE 17:12–19

Happy Mother's Day! You won't be surprised that today's sermon is especially aimed at mothers. Now, if you are not a mother, please don't feel excluded. There is much in the scripture for today that is important for all of us to hear. In fact, there is no mention of motherhood in this text. It's just that there is something in the story that I think is particularly important for those (mothers or fathers or grandparents or caregivers or teachers or nurses) who have as a part of their daily task the care and feeding and loving and molding of others.

And the question that the text raises is this: How do we, amidst our busy and demanding lives, stay centered, focused, inspired for the hard work that we do? I suspect that you are like me: I consider it a wonderful privilege to serve God by trying to make a difference in God's world. Don't you? Most of the time, my work with people and with my family provides such joy that when people ask, "What keeps you going? What inspires you?" it seems like a silly question. The sheer joy of the work does.

Jesus had many teachings about what his disciples were to do to make a difference in the world: clothe the naked, feed the hungry, visit those in prison, give hope to the hopeless. Those are the obvious passages that we as Christians use for inspiration for making the world a better place. But there are days, aren't there, when the work is not quite enough, when the chaos out there hooks the chaos in here and it is hard, very hard, to stay centered or to even remember why it is we do what we do.

But there is this story from the gospel of Luke that helps me in this regard. It's not one of the passages we would perhaps look to first for inspiration. It's an unusual story in many ways. But it is one of my favorites. It's the story of Jesus and the ten lepers. Listen to it with me. (Luke 17:12–19 is read.)

7

One reason I love this story is that there is room for everybody here to climb inside it. Most of the stories about people who encounter Jesus are about an individual person. But this story stands by itself in being not about a single individual but about a group who are standing in a circle together because they are standing in a *common need*. This little congregation of ten may be made up of very different individuals, but they can stand together now because they know they all need something. And they look at Jesus from a distance and wave and say, "Lord, have mercy. Help us."

The name of their particular disease is leprosy, one of the most feared diseases of Jesus' day. Many have made the connection between leprosy and HIV/AIDS in our day. It would have had the same social connotations that HIV/AIDS or the rampant disease of unwed mothers do in our politics today. But the name of the need isn't really what matters. What matters is *how many of us* have such a need, how many of us belong in the company of those who are calling for help…and not just as helpers. One of the things we who are seeking to change the world for the better often lack is the recognition that *we are every bit as needy as the world.* One of the dangers of being helpers and healers making a difference in the world is that—so in touch are we with the pain all around us—we forget our own hurt, our own real needs. One of the things we must acknowledge if we are to remain inspired in our work, one of the things we must admit in order to stay centered as mothers, fathers, helpers, teachers, caregivers—is that we belong in *that circle of need.*

So, if there is any sadness pressing against your heart today, you belong in that circle. If you've got some guilt that you cannot seem to get rid of, you belong. If your soul is tired or confused or scared and lonely, you're in the group. If you are right now in the middle of a hard decision you don't know how to make, you're in. It doesn't have to be you that's on your mind. It could be someone else you care about who's in trouble, and you'd do anything to help but you don't know how to help: If so, you have a place, too, in the circle of those of us who cry for mercy.

People in that circle don't have to feel close to Jesus. You don't have to be a part of the church community. You may be wrestling right now with profound doubts about your faith. You still belong. You can still find your center in this circle. The folks in the circle in

Luke's story were not close to Jesus. Nor were they members of any church. They stood off in the distance, a long way off from the pious and the organized. But they were part of the circle. So welcome to the circle, whoever you are, whatever the current state of your heart. Raise your hand with the rest of us and call out your need. I'm here in this circle too. We can call out together, "Hey Lord, have mercy. Do you see us over here? Will you have mercy?"

I hope you don't mind who else is with you in that group. This is something that we owe to each other *and* to our world: that we don't mind too much who else is in the circle with us, calling on God. Recognizing your own pain and hurt can put you in very different company from what you have been used to. That's the thing about leprosy. When the doctor diagnoses you a leper, you lose all your old memberships. In Jesus' time, a leper couldn't stay where he or she used to belong. No more family. No more job. No more club meetings. They were required to leave their place, their positions, all their relationships and wander on the outside of things. Lepers in the gospels stand for all who have lost their old identities, their smug place in the world, their illusions of being "in" and have found themselves in the much simpler membership in the fellowship of pain, which is not very exclusive company.

In the particular group of ten about which Luke tells are some folks who used to mistrust each other, who would not have lowered themselves to talk to each other. In that circle are old racial enemies: Samaritans and Jews. But it's funny how all those old divisions don't matter any more. They don't matter when you know that where you really belong is in the fellowship of need and suffering. One of the most inclusive and warm groups that I know is Narcotics Anonymous. Black, white, women, men, gay, straight, rich, poor—all can stand in the circle of need and cry for help. I hope you don't mind too much who you stand beside when you ask for help…including fundamentalists…and liberals…and bigots…and rednecks…and drunks…and people who smell like a whole lot of money…and people who smell like the streets. If you don't mind who you stand with in this circle, then your need has probably taught you well enough to raise your hand with the rest of us and say, "Me too!" And if you have ever wondered why the church is full of so many imperfect people, so many hypocrites and sinners—this is why—they all stand in this circle of need, with more questions than answers, with flaws and wounds—just like you.

Jesus gives an answer to these people who cry from a distance. But to people like us, his answer is really a shock, because he doesn't say anything like, "Children, I know how much it hurts…" or "Tell me more about your pain…" He doesn't say a tender word. He doesn't even come a step closer to them. He doesn't touch them or tell them, "Now, I've healed you." All he says is *"Go!"* And it sounds like a stern command. *"Go!"* Jesus never did take that training course in clinical pastoral education—or he flunked it. Sometimes you come to the center to get comfort, and what you get is a commandment.

Has that ever happened to you when you have gone to church? Something in your world has just devastated you, and you come seeking a center, wounded, dragging yourself limping into worship because you need some word of comfort and hope…and the sermon is a call to give more of your money? Don't you just hate it when that happens? What this story suggests is that sometimes the need for healing is not best answered with soft words…but is best answered with the hearing and obeying of a new commandment.

"Go and show yourselves to the priests," he says. Now that's what a leper did *after* he had been healed. He went to the priest, who checked him over and told him he was all right. These ten are not cured. But Jesus commands them to act *as if* they were cured. He won't hand them a healing, but he will give them something to do on faith. In other words, he'll honor them with a partnership in their own healing. And that is the meaning of all of God's commandments; all of what we call *the law* is really God's gracious insistence that we take the steps that are *our part* in getting well.

These ten decide to trust the grace of a commandment. Uncured, they act as if they might be—by being obedient. And what do you know, what do you know, when they go and do what they were commanded, they discover that they are all wearing new skin. One reason I like this story so much is that it is much more like the experiences I have with healing. Some of the gospel stories seem to imply that a healing from God comes instantly. But most of us don't get better all of a sudden. And most of the people we work with certainly don't get healthy all at once. Real transformations almost always occur somewhere down the road, somewhere between a word we heard and our destination. We'd like to be fixed right now. We'd like to fix the world right now. But the fixing almost always happens down the road of being faithful.

In *Pilgrim's Progress,* old Christian has a burden on his back. He hates the burden on his back, and he's trying to get rid of it. A guy named Evangelist says, "What you need to do is go way up there to that little wicket gate." So Christian does go way up there. He runs and he walks and he crawls. He finally reaches the gate, but the burden is still on his back. He asks, "Why is this burden still on my back?" And his host says, "As to the burden, be content to bear it, until thou comest to the place of Deliverance; for there it will fall from thy back it self."[3] Farther down the road, it does. The word of God isn't magical. We keep wishing that it were, but it's not. The word of God itself does not heal us. The word of God sends us on the path where the healing overtakes us if we'll go.

It happens to the ten, a healing on the way. Somewhere along the way of going where they were commanded, they discover that their hands and feet and faces have put on new skin. Leprosy really is an awful disease—rotting skin on living humans. And here their flesh is restored—fresh as a child's perfect, unblemished skin. Don't you know they were ecstatic? Can't you see the high-fives? Can't you hear the "Yes!" And they do what I think just about any of us would do when headed down the highway with a brand-new life. They accelerate. Jesus had told them to go. Going made them better. What are new feet for, if not to sprint to the finish of what we've been told to do? "Go to the priests then, and step on it!"

Except for one of them. One of the ten breaks stride, slows down, stops, then turns completely around. He is suddenly in no hurry to see his priest. He's got something wilder than compliance on his mind. He's got a new skin. He's got a new life. This needs and wants a new voice—gotta do something here! So he runs the other way, praising God, says Luke, with a loud voice and then falling at the feet of Jesus, saying, "Thank you. Thank you! Thank you!!" You can bet it wasn't a tidy little thank you speech either. I bet he didn't have a manuscript. I bet it was a halting, stammering babble and a puddle of tears in the dust.

Paul Duke says that the praise of God is the improvisation in the jazz of worship.[4] Improvisation is when the music takes you, and you do what you need to do and play what you need to play, not because the musical score commands it, but because your own soul commands it, in response to the music. The praise of God is the improvisation in the jazz of worship.

Here Luke breaks in to add a piece of information we haven't had until now. That tenth leper was a Samaritan. Oh. He has been cleansed from the stigma of disease, but he's still wearing the stigma of race for a whole lot of people. All through his life he's going to be an outcast—cured or not. But it is he, the outcast, who has come back to pour out his praise. Why is that? Why do you think it is that so many of the marginalized people of our society express more freedom in their worship than do those who never question that they are in the "in" group? Why is it that members of churches on the poorer side of town, largely African American churches or Latino churches or poor white Pentecostal churches, exhibit so much more joy and freedom in their worship than those of us of the solidly middle class? What do the shut out and the put down know about praise that some of the rest of us don't? That's what Jesus wants us to think about now.

Jesus says, "Mmm, weren't there ten? Where are the nine?" Well there's a perfectly obvious answer to that question. The nine are out doing exactly what Jesus told them to do. They are doing their duty. They've taken the road as commanded. They've gotten better on the road. And they seem to think that staying on the road is the thing. They're like Forrest Gump with a football. They've crossed the goal. And they keep right on running, clear out of the stadium where a celebration happens without them.

Maybe part of what keeps these guys running is their eagerness to be certified. That's what the priests are going to give them, you know. And with their certification of cure, all their memberships will be reinstated, they'll be able to be a volunteer with Mother to Mother and not "just" a client. Maybe a Samaritan, an outcast, knows not to trust that stuff so much. Maybe he knows that the establishment can't give him anything that matters. Maybe he knows that everything that matters, he's already been given. And he also knows what time it is. It's doxology time. It's praise music time. It's time to let loose with love and unnecessary song. It's time to find the way to say love and say thanks. It's time to give beauty, beauty, beauty back to God.[5]

And here's the thing: Until we find ourselves there, we don't find ourselves whole. As a church, as individuals, we can run down the road of doing all the right things for the world—and of course we ought to do them! Feed the hungry. Clothe the naked. Visit the imprisoned. Mother our children well. Provide a whole village ready to raise our children. We owe the world these things. But while doing these as commanded will make you better, they will not make you *whole,* they will not make you centered until you come to the place of wild, gratuitous praise. Jesus gave ten healings that day. Everybody got new skin. But it was the one who poured out praise at his feet— that one heard him say, "Your faith has made you whole."

Jesus requires obedience in his command to love the world. That's the necessary half. But he loves the unnecessary half—where we run back to the feet of God and improvise our own expressions of love and praise. These the world needs too. Sometimes I think we, as the church, look for all the world like nine dutiful lepers, trying to do the right thing. Half-whole people trying to do the right stuff to get someone's approval still. Where's the *one* who wheels around for the wildness of love's beauty in return? The world needs that too!

Here we come to the awkward place, though. For if I try to give you specific ways in which to whirl around to give spontaneous beauty back to God, it's going to sound like the language of commandment, when what we need to experience is our freedom to give what is not commanded. Had Jesus told the ten, "You guys come back and give thanks," they would have done it. But they would not have been made whole. No one can tell you what to do out of gratitude, and without gratitude there is no center. I can tell you what to do out of duty—and would that more of us would do our duty. But what might you improvise for the world out of gratitude for what you've been given?

Well, let me try to stimulate your imaginations with some improvisations of my own—not in the language of commandment, but as examples of what you might, in your freedom, offer to God and God's world. The next time you find yourself overwhelmingly grateful for a friendship you are in, for the love of someone who is there for you, who has cared for you and comforted you and made you laugh, and made you think...the next time that happens, why not improvise some completely unnecessary and unexpected way to say thank you to her and to God? Or the next time a new idea strikes you with the force of new freedom, or you realize how important your work is to you and how much joy it gives you, why not improvise some completely unnecessary and unexpected way to say thank you to God for ideas that liberate and work that is important? There is a preacher's phrase going around the church these days. It's an attempt to respond to random acts of violence. Some preachers are advocating random acts of kindness. Well, that feels a bit trite to me—but it's kind of what I'm getting at here. Improvise the unnecessary and unexpected out of gratitude to God. You may not *owe* it to the world. But the world desperately needs it. And it will make God smile to see the one who stops on the busy road and turns to offer such unexpected praise. Offer beauty, beauty, beauty. Joy, joy, joy. That's when you will be fully centered in the gospel of our Lord Jesus Christ. Thanks be to God!

CHAPTER 2

Teresa L. Fry
Brown

Although I have taught preaching for fourteen and a half years, examining my own creative process is one of the most difficult undertakings I have encountered. Self-reflection can be both painful and nourishing. Although my profession involves listening to other preachers and helping them in "finding their own voice," I rarely assess my own methods. I have become self-assured that if I do proper preparation and yield myself to God, the sermon will develop. It took ten years to find my preaching voice, style, and particular peculiar preparation journey. I constantly adjust and hone my preaching skills through reading, listening, and practice. I preach approximately once or twice a week. The preaching moment takes place at various denominational worship services, revivals, conferences, and workshops. There have been weeks when I have preached each day and have known that the Spirit of God allowed me to preach a fresh word each day. It is only through the indwelling of that same Spirit that I am able to delineate my own creative preaching process in four areas: preparation, delivery, feedback, and experiential transformation.

Conception and Gestation

Preaching is one of the most exciting activities in my life. The thought that God has chosen me to deliver the Word is overwhelming. I do not take the privilege lightly. Preparation always begins with prayer and personal devotion time. I ask God what I am to preach. I realize that preaching is a God-ordained event and that my mind is not intelligent enough to know what needs to be imparted at any one time. I rely on my spiritual connection with God to determine the text and form of the sermon. I try to vary the form—topically, textually, narratively, rhetorically, and so forth—so that I am not bound in predictability. I usually use an Old Testament and New Testament text in each sermon in order to demonstrate the connection of prophecy and fulfillment. This means extensive study so that the connection is natural and not contrived. I consider with whom I am to preach and study the lives of the listeners. If I am a guest preacher, I talk with the pastor or someone at the church to get a general idea of the congregational ecology. I pray for illumination about the needs of the people with whom I am to preach. I look for universal needs, issues, theologies, cultures, and biblical literacy. This enables me to preach with the people and not over, around, or under their level of need and understanding. I "listen" for the rhythms of life, observe current affairs, ask questions of the text, and reflect on my personal needs and those of possible listeners—the condition of the human family.

My initial preparation stage is a slow burn. It is as if my mind is on simmer. I feel something within, but it is in that nebulous part of me just beyond reach. It is like the early stages of a pregnancy or after seeds have been planted. I know there is new life, but I cannot locate it in the ultrasound of my mind. Over a period of minutes or days the sermon ideas begin to bounce around like mental popcorn. It is awesome and exhilarating. I write as fast as I can and try to organize the ideas into an outline of similar points. The next stage is deep thought. It is as if God needs to take me into the wilderness or off on a island away from the mundane so I can fully attend to spiritual instructions. I have to be alone for about an hour to concentrate on the particular preaching moment. Sometimes I have to go for a drive, walk around outside, sit quietly, or sing in order to be focused. Other times I have to go watch television, see a movie, or be around a lot of people in order for the sermon to germinate. I leave the notes alone for a day and go back to them when I "hear" God say that it's time to go write.

I do not have a regular schedule for when I write. I use time in supermarket lines, traffic, school meetings, and church services to note new sermon ideas or "spiritual moments." For the past fifteen or sixteen years I have kept a notepad by my bed, in the bathroom, in my purse, on my desks, in the kitchen, and in the car as homiletical resource files. When I listen to others preach, I find myself jotting down notes of what to do and what not to do in the preaching event. I am more often than not inspired when I hear what God is doing through others in their songs, prayers, testimonies, sermons, or life experiences.

I grew up in a household where reading all types of literature, singing all types of music, conversing with a variety of persons, worshiping across denominations, working with all age groups, and building inclusive community were paramount. This is reflected in my preaching preparation. I am called to preach with all persons, regardless of their nation or station in life. There is no area of knowledge or experience that I exclude from my possible homiletical resources. I was taught that everything God made was good and for a purpose. I try to learn something from everyone and everything and look for application in a particular biblical text. Lived experience— factual or fictional—enhances the relevance of the biblical text.

My exegetical process begins with asking questions of the text— who, what, when, where, how, why—and what God wants us to know about application of the text. I read the entire chapter of a text as well as the preceding and following chapters, if possible. I look for connections between related Old Testament and New Testament texts. I compare and contrast five to seven translations [KJV, NKJV, NIV, NRSV, TEV, ASV, or *The Message*] of a stipulated text to determine which works for that particular sermon. I consult dictionaries, thesauruses, word studies, concordances, maps, cultural analysis, historical studies, and anthropology. I consult commentaries as a conversation partner only after my first outline or draft of the text is in place in my head or on paper. I use the same writing organizational format I learned in sixth-grade English—thesis statement, introduction, body paragraphs, transition statements, and conclusion. This allows me to have a coherent, logical sermon and lessens the temptation to ramble. I rarely use stories or jokes. I find that too many stories distract from the biblical text. I am not a joke teller, although I do insert spur-of-the-moment quips from time to time.

I fell in love with language as a child. My mother required us to go to the library and read on many Saturday mornings. She believed in the power of knowledge. We were encouraged to read and memorize all types of literature from a variety of cultures. Even now I read one book not directly related to theology per week. The flow of language, the sight of the written word on paper is powerful. My homiletical resources include poetry, prose, music, medical research, science, mathematics, alliterations, word play, and Hebrew, Greek, Latin, and English definitions. I do constant Bible study so that I am familiar with many passages. I teach Bible studies, Christian Education workshops, and preaching conferences, which forces me to continue in-depth study of the biblical text. This is a time saver in sermon preparation and extemporaneous delivery.

I rarely preach from the lectionary. I think it is a good resource for preachers to focus on texts some would avoid. When I receive invitations from Episcopal or United Methodist churches, I consult the lectionary so I will have an idea of the general service content. I may use one of the readings or find a similar text for the sermon. I think it is vitally important for the sermon to mesh with the totality of the worship service. It is not the star vehicle but a part of the worship service.

I do not avoid controversial subjects. I believe it is my task to challenge the preacher and the people to move toward transformation and live in the conversion. I believe it is a cardinal homiletical sin to preach a soft sermon that does not incite some type of action. All sermons should impart some new insight on the biblical text. The sermons I write are packed with didache (teaching) as well as kerygma (language about the prophecy, birth, ministry, death, resurrection, and parousia of Jesus). I remain open to the Spirit to illuminate the people whether the text is lectionary- or Spirit-led and fed.

I know that my preaching passion is social justice and transformation. These core values are inherent in each sermon I preach.

Text selection is a result of prayer, spiritual guidance, occasion, sermon purpose, and cultural imperatives. I have files of sermons that were written but never delivered. Over the years I have decided that these are sermons God sends as a way of preparing me, pruning me, cleansing me for my conduit experience. The conduit experience means that Teresa is not the preacher; she is just a vessel that the sermon passes through from God to the people. It is not unusual for me to finish the written portion of the sermon as I begin to stand up to deliver it. I do not think that a sermon is ever complete. I pray to remain open to the Holy Spirit's creative insights.

I write a draft of a phrase sermon and read over it a couple of times to make sure it makes sense. I then ask myself questions as if I were the person in the pews and need a word to apply to my current struggles. I understand that the sermon is for me as well as the congregation. I jot down scenarios of relief for difficulty and parallel the biblical text resolution to contemporary resolution. I again leave the sermon manuscript and do other activities. I write the sermon in longhand on five-by-eight inch cards rather than typing because my perfectionist personality demands minimal errors. Seeing the red underscore on a computer breaks my concentration. The flow of pen to paper is the center of my creative outpouring. It is as if the thoughts flow from my brain, down my arm, through the pen, and onto the paper. I normally spend an average of forty to fifty preparation hours per sermon. I validate that each second of my life has prepared me for the next preaching moment. There have been occasions where I was asked to preach with five minutes' notice. I sat still, took a deep breath, prayed for a text, and got up and preached twenty-five minutes. I believe that each preacher always has a sermon ready to share with others. The length and depth totally depend on God's direction and the preacher's obedience to the Spirit of illumination.

I write constantly throughout the week or weeks before the sermon. I write notes, words, sentences, ancillary ideas, what the text reminds me of in real life, thoughts about how I can use information in a different context, and what I am sensing as I read the text. I attend to ideas or words that jump out of the text in several readings and translations. I consider textual punctuation, background material, color, sounds, emotion, consequences, actions, personalities, conflict, age, occupation, familial structure, attitudes, relationships, tastes, and movement. I analyze the presence, activity, love, judgment, and intervention of God, Jesus the Christ, and the Holy Spirit. My general writing composition time is erratic. I usually have the premise or topic in mind early in the week. If I am preaching a special worship service, revival, or conference, I know the general theme at least a month to a year ahead of time. This does not always result in a sermon on that theme. I have tried to write the final draft early in the week or day, but am unable to do so. I think about what the sermon involves— topic, exegesis of the text, introduction, body, conclusion, and so forth—but have been unable to put it down on paper until God gives me the signal. Often by the time the day comes around, God has given me something else to preach.

Labor and Delivery

Crunch time for a Sunday sermon is between 9:00 p.m. Saturday and 5:00 a.m. Sunday. My most productive time is 2:00 a.m. to 5:00 a.m. on Sunday. My energy level is high, and the house is quiet. I can hear clearly then, and the Spirit waters my soul like moisture in a dry sponge. When the sermon is finally down on paper, I am both exhilarated and tired. It is like finishing an exercise routine. I know that the workout increased my heart rate and my health, yet my body is screaming for some rest. Physically I am drained, but mentally I am ready to preach. Often I have prayed for a 5:00 a.m. service so I can give birth to the sermon in the congregation.

I am a full manuscript writer, but I do not read the sermon verbatim. I have always been a multi-sensory person, whether I am singing, sewing, cooking, or preaching. I try to use action verbs, descriptive nouns, and colorful adverbs or adjectives to enhance the "sensory-feel" of the sermon. My goal is to allow the listener to become a part of the sermon. The listener should be able to see himself/herself as part of the story. There must be a connection made with the biblical story and the contemporary situation. I have found that flat, unimaginative language is psychically monotone. Too many "touchy-feely" stories or exclusive jokes place the listener on the outside of the sermon. I want the listeners to become a part of the sermon. I strive to be so concise and clear that they visualize the hope that comes from belief and are actually part of the old, old story and see new possibilities for their lives. The more sensory input, the more persons remember the content and intent of the sermon.

I cannot clearly identify hindrances to developing a sermon. So-called difficult texts inspire me to study more and look for a nuance that I have not considered before. I like to take familiar texts and preach them in new ways. In my culture there are traditional preaching texts, such as the parting of the Red Sea, the Hebrew men in the furnace, Daniel in the lions' den, the valley of dry bones, the raising of Lazarus, the woman with the issue of blood, or the revelatory nations ascending into heaven. I approach the texts with different lenses, yet honoring my tradition, I strive to preach a different aspect of the text.

As I said before, all of life informs the next sermon assignment. I look forward to preaching. I am both challenged and honored by a time to preach. I accept all preaching engagements, whether there are two people or ten thousand. I have preached in all denominations ecumenically and participated in worship at a synagogue, in hospitals, on the beach, in the back yard, in fellowship halls, in hotels, in restaurants, on the sidewalk, in the grocery store line, in the parking lot, at military installations, and at hospices. My daughter informs me that I preach around the house, at Bible study, and in the car. I see sermon material everywhere and marvel at what God created. I try to see the good in all situations and find sermon material in assets and liabilities.

There are times when the sound system is poor, the fire alarm goes off, people get sick, babies cry, the temperature is unbearable, my allergies act up, or I am not well, but the sermon goes on regardless. I have learned to make adjustments and let God do the rest. If in the middle of the sermon God says stop, I find a way to end the sermon and sit down. Flexibility is the key to handling distractions or hindrances. I do not turn down a preaching engagement unless I am so ill I cannot stand up. Earlier in my career I did not preach in places where I was not allowed in the pulpit. After about four years I realized that all ground is holy ground and that it did not matter where I stood as long as God's Word went forth.

When I am ill, God gives me preaching ideas. When I am driving, traffic inspires me. I used to direct gospel choirs, and the melody of all forms of music inspires me. I use all experiences—flat tires, sports, illnesses, recipes, conversations, newspapers, Internet, movies, songs, commercials, elders, children, animals, MTV, BET, CNN, plants, shapes, clouds, natural disasters, sounds, silence, newscasts, and so forth—as supportive illustrations. I do not own a book of illustrations or stories for sermons. I feel that God has enough of them in day-to-day life. The most critical exegesis tools I possess are my eyes and ears. The most critical preparation tools are my senses. The most critical creative tools for me are God and the world around me.

Prior to the preaching moment I have undergone a process of self-exegesis. Who's Teresa today? How do I feel? What have I noticed about myself? What is God saying in this time? Am I physically, emotionally, spiritually, psychologically equipped to deliver the sermon God has placed in my heart? I dream about delivery of the sermon. I see the faces of the people, hear my voice, feel how my body moves, hear God speaking, and even smell the anticipation of hope. There have been times when I have envisioned the angelic host within the congregation helping me preach. I think about all the women and men who were unable to preach due to social restrictions, and I am encouraged to preach with God's power. Because there are still vestiges of society where my sisters' voices are muted, I try all the more to be a preacher of integrity, courage, and preparation.

I like to sit quietly and just observe the congregation prior to the sermon. I think that it is imperative for the preacher to attend the entire worship service to feel the vibes of the people. I may attend an earlier worship service or Sunday school class so I can learn about the local theology. I engage the environment to hear where the people are in their faith development, to sense the mood of the people, and to test the emotional climate of the day. When possible, I arrive early enough to test the microphone, the acoustics, the size and shape of the preaching space, the height of the podium, and the pulpit and congregational seating.

I try to have minimal conversation to conserve my voice and listen to last-minute instructions from God. I rarely sleep before a sermon and never eat prior to preaching. I sip only room temperature water, just enough to moisten my mouth. I try to wear comfortable clothes and minimal jewelry. As a woman who happens to preach, I do not think I need to look, act, or sound like a man who happens to preach. I enjoy my particularity and know that God chose me to preach as Teresa—called, chosen, ordained, anointed, and appointed by God. Earlier in my preaching career I was told to wear only dark clothes, flat shoes, no makeup, hair pulled back or cut short, and no jewelry, so I would look like a preacher. I was encouraged to use a deep voice and not sing as part of the preaching moment. God and I decided that that was another way to keep women from being fully who God made us. So I now wear a robe when I feel it is appropriate. I have an array of robes and Afrocentric preaching attire. I wear dark clothing when my fashion sense and reverence says it is appropriate. I wear suits or dresses that are appropriate to my size and shape. I love rich vibrant colors. I see no reason to put a covering on my head or my lap. That, in my mind, harks back to the Corinthians passage about head coverings and wanton women. It alludes to women's so-called ability to "entice" men, as if men had no responsibility to keep their eyes and minds on God and not on people. I take my high-heeled shoes off when I preach because I feel comfortable on holy ground. I wear my hair in braids or hanging on my shoulders, depending on my mood. I wear makeup and jewelry. I think that I am intelligent enough to know what is appropriate and what is not. I do not wear clerical collars, pink, hats, or frills. Those items work for some women but not for me. The bottom line is that the Word spoken should be more important than the appearance of the vessel. No one has ever been saved by how attractive or unattractive the preacher was.

In the process of preaching I try to look at the listeners, notice if they are following points, and note body language. I handle distractions by either ignoring them or incorporating them into the sermon on the spur of the moment. I use voice modulation and inflection to vary my vocal production. I have a "preaching voice," but I do not know how to describe it. There seems to be another voice inside me that is birthed once I begin to preach. It leaves when the sermon is over. The average time of preaching is thirty-five minutes. I have preached as short as one minute and as long as fifty. Length depends on the movement of the Spirit and the occasion. As I stated before, I write a full manuscript but rarely read it. I am open to new insights that occur as I preach. There have been instances when I read none of the manuscript and other times when another sermon formed as I stood to preach. My delivery begins slowly, and then the momentum of the sermon builds to the ending. I always end with a note of hope for the listener.

Over the years my style has become freer. When I began preaching seventeen years or so ago, I was tied to the manuscript. I over-researched and thought I had to read it all. Now I do the same amount of research, but I do a much more efficient job of editing. I never preach the same sermon the same way twice. If I preach back-to-back services, I know that the people are different—and so am I. God's copy editor does the work. I also now realize that there are no perfect sermons. Everyone has a bad day now and then regardless of the amount of preparation. Sometimes it is something within the preacher, sometimes within the congregation.

The need to be perfect is a deadly element of preaching. As long as I have taken the time to prepare, I know that I am there to please God and not the people. I do not seek external praise. My job is to preach a good, saving, transforming word, not to please the people. There are still persons who want women to "preach like men." That is anathema to me. I believe that God chooses each of us as individual vessels, and therefore we each should have our own style and sound. I know now when I am trying to force my agenda on a sermon and when God says no. I have learned that when I hear "stop" or "no" in my head, it means that I should choose a different way of saying or doing whatever is at hand.

Feedback and Aftercare

Feedback is critical for development as a preacher. Self-critique is difficult but required. We each know when we have done our best and when we were ill-prepared. Constructive criticism is a building block for better preaching. I have three preaching partners in different parts of the country. One is African Methodist Episcopal, one is Baptist, and one is United Methodist. We bounce sermon ideas off one another, and at times I read portions of a sermon for response. I trust them enough to "speak the truth in love." If I am focusing on youth, I ask for my daughter's perspective on issues facing younger people and the language of the day. I discuss embryonic sermon ideas with my husband, Bible study group, and prayer partners. I also review similar sermons I have heard or preached to stimulate ideas for how to improve the next time I preach.

Feedback during the preaching moment is like a natural high. I am able to transition, add points of information, connect with the listeners, be open to the indwelling direction of the Holy Spirit, and spread my homiletical wings as the rhythms of the speaker and listener are in sync, driving the sermon. In my culture, verbal feedback ("Amen") and physical feedback (claps, foot stomps, standing up, dancing) are immediate. When I preach in other cultural or denominational settings, I rely on eye contact, body language, and comments after the service. My family or friends also assist in feedback for pacing or approval of points during and after the preaching moment.

I take about thirty minutes after the sermon, usually on the way home, to quietly thank God for bringing me through another opportunity to preach, and reflect on what happened. If I have preached and have a lengthy trip home, I use the time of the flight or driving to review the sermon and replay it in my head. This is a rich time for me as I marvel at what was on the paper and what God did during the preaching moment. It takes about two hours for me to "come down" after I have preached. I review my audio and videotapes once a month. I also keep track of what sermons were preached when and where and how I can improve them. I refilter sermons before I use them again and make adjustments accordingly. Occasionally I go back to sermons I wrote years ago and compare and contrast them to current ones to chart my growth and development as a preacher. I am grateful to God for change and improvement. I realize there is still much to learn. My creative process is still evolving.

The following sermon, *A Love Letter Written in Blood,* was prepared for a Maundy Thursday service at Ebenezer Baptist Church in Atlanta, Georgia. At the invitation of Rev. Joseph Roberts, pastor, I was a part of the Lenten Worship Series 2000. Although I had two months' notice, other responsibilities and an illness prevented me from working on the sermon or writing it until the morning it was to be delivered. I had preached during Lent before, but never on Maundy Thursday. I also had to preach the next night in Good Friday worship and at a week-long revival the next week. Several sermons were floating through my head for all seven engagements. There are several texts listed in the lectionary for Maundy Thursday. I prayed for the one that would be most appropriate for Ebenezer. The service was to end with a communion ritual. I asked my students to describe the worship experience there. I knew the history of Ebenezer as the Martin Luther

King family church. I had never attended worship there but trusted that the Lord would direct my path.

A Love Letter Written in Blood
LUKE 22:14–20

"How do I love thee? Let me count the ways."[1]

Elizabeth Barrett Browning's often-quoted classic poem tells of the depth of human love. We live in a world replete with declarations of love, searches for love, absence of love, abuse of love, and denial of love. Look around us. We cheer Tina Turner's resolve in "What's Love Got to Do with It?" We fail, however, to ask why Ike Turner thought it was all right to abuse her in the name of love. Fifty percent of marriages last in spite of infidelity, sickness, debt, children's needs, and lack of employment, while many people leave a committed relationship as soon as lust cools down. Families are decimated when one member decides that suicide is the answer, leaving lives littered listlessly in valleys of despair. Our young people are taught by media and the morose models of some adults that the best demonstration of love is physical union and not unity of hearts, souls, and minds. When we feel as if we are unloved or can't seem to love ourselves, we seek quick fixes in drugs, ego, violence, shopping, power games, and ego trips to stop the pain. Hallmark, Mahogany, and American Greeting cards cannot create a means to stop the counterfeit love that pervades our reality.

Beloved, I stopped by to share God's message about true love. God arranged to send us a love letter that covers our needs, desires, and wants. This letter speaks of an intimacy and relationship that we will never lose. This letter is about a love that is faithful, true, and death defying.

Walk back with me for a short time to our stated text for this evening. The Lukan passage is a part of Jesus' farewell discourse. The parade is over. The palm branches from three days ago are now trampled in the dust. The fig tree has been cursed. The Pharisees have plotted to kill this man named Jesus because they fear they will lose some of their power. The people have begun to emerge from darkness into a marvelous light. Jesus has wept over Jerusalem. Judas has already agreed to a $13.20 bounty to tell them where Jesus is staying. Over 200,000 extra folk are in Jerusalem to pay their eighty-cent temple tax and give their sin offerings. Jesus has shut down the money-changers' flea market. Mary has already poured out her oil from the alabaster box. Now the disciples gather in the upper room with Jesus.

The disciples have spent three long years with Jesus. Now Jesus is eager to meet privately with his friends just one more time. Peter and John have prepared the meal. At the time of the meal the other disciples are told which house to go to for dinner. Usually dinner or supper is the last meal of the evening. For Passover, the last meal had to be eaten between 6:00 (sundown) and midnight (start of a new day). The Passover meal was one of three compulsory meals required by Jews during the year.

Beginning at verse 14—When the hour came, the kairos, Jesus took his place at the long wooden table with thirteen reclining seats. He said to them, "I have eagerly desired to eat this Passover meal with you before I suffer. This is the last time I will have an opportunity to eat with you." Can you imagine the disciples, the grief in the room, the stomachs churning, the heads throbbing? I imagine they said, "We have been together three years as students, as sojourners, as your friends. What do you mean this is the last time?" Jesus takes on the responsibility of serving the meal, taking the role as the oldest in the room, and answers them by demonstration.

This meal was different; Jesus did not drink the wine. As we look at verse 17, Jesus took the cup (the third cup) and he blessed it. He gave it to the disciples and told them to drink it. He said, "I will not drink the Passover wine until I come back, until the fruit of the vine ripens. I will not share the drink until the future restoration, the new covenant, God's plan, promise, power, and purpose is done."

Then the Bible says he took the bread and broke it. It doesn't say he cut it or sliced it or tore it. It says Jesus broke the bread. The bread represents the body, the spiritual nourishment we need for life. It represents the breaking of chains of slavery of sin and sin of slavery. It means deliverance from habits, addictions, and excess emotional, mental, and physical baggage. Jesus said, "Do this!" It was not a suggestion. It was a command, an order. Take this cup. Break this bread. Eat together. No divisions, come together. No need to push and shove. Come together and eat. The disciples that night had been trying to see who was the greatest, but Jesus says all are equal. Some of us are like the disciples at the meal. Some of us are angry when we come to the table. We are more interested in where we sit than what we take into our bodies. Some of us have betrayed God by whoring after other gods. Some of us have taken the meal mouthing "thank you" but with no love in our hearts. Some of us have eaten the meal just so others can see that we are present. But Jesus says, "Take the cup, take the bread in remembrance of who I am and who you can become." Do all of it to remember what sacrifice Jesus was about to make and had made for us.

"Do this in remembrance of me. Not yourselves, but me." Remembrance is anamnesis. Jesus knows that we get busy sometimes and forget how we got over, who paved the way for us, who rescued us, who sacrificed for us, who fought for us, and who died for us. We get so encased in our titles, our jobs, our spouses, our children, our clubs, our social standing, our political stances, our education, our financial plans, our sports, our church, that we forget God. We get selective amnesia and think that we are God. We begin to practice functional atheism and believe that all things come from us instead of from God. Jesus presents a tangible means for remembering who we are and whose we are. Do this in remembrance of me.

As we approach verse 20, Jesus takes the fourth cup, after supper, and says, "This cup is poured out for you. It is the new covenant, new agreement, new contract, new relationship, new testament, a new will. This cup is the symbol of my love for you. *It is my blood.*" The entire purpose of the meal is to recognize the new commandment written in blood. It is to look backward and reflect on Jesus' sacrifice. It is to look forward and see the fulfillment of the kingdom of God. It is to look inward to go through self-examination of how we have all sinned and come short of God's glory. It is a look upward to imagine the Savior now seated at the right hand of God, interceding for us. It is a look outward so that we understand that the sacrifice was for the whole world because God loved the entire world, not just me, mine, and my.

Jesus tells us that the new commandment will keep us safe from hurt, harm, and danger. The new commandment is written in Jesus' blood and symbolizes his love for each of us. This new covenant is about the forgiveness of sin. No need for doves or lambs; Jesus became the sin offering. He is worth more than eighty cents and certainly more than the $13.20 Judas sold him for that night. Jesus has presented his body for us. Jesus said, "This is my blood. It is the seal of the covenant. This is the new commandment. I know I gave ten to Moses and spoke about two others last year, but this is the one I am leaving with you: Love one another."

"Love one another as I have loved you. Love all people as I have loved you. Love within the group you know, and love all those you will meet. This is the reason, the purpose I came. I came to teach you to love—agape love. If you love me, keep my commandments. If you love me, change your ways. Stop lying. Get rid of your anger. Watch how you talk. Pay attention to where you walk. Stop stealing. Stop breaking God's heart. Forgive one another. Honor god with your talents. Love god. If you love me…How do you love me? Greater love has no one than this. I will lay down my life for you. But you have to love one another."

This new covenant is not signed with ink made from fish, plants, crushed shells, or synthetics. This covenant, this letter, this agreement is signed in blood. It has special properties designed and created by God. The purpose of blood is to give nutrients to our physical system. It is necessary for reproduction, growth, and cleansing our systems of toxins. A lack of blood leads to anemia, rupture, and disease. There is no energy, no strength, no power without blood. There are only six quarts of blood in the human body, but this blood is plentiful enough to keep all of humanity alive. The blood of this covenant condemns, convinces, convicts, converts, counsels, covers, consecrates, and commissions us for service to God. This blood helps rid us of malice, greed, sloth, slander, lying tongues, killing hands, wicked hearts, haughty eyes, false witness, and destructive actions. This blood is poured out, poured out, poured out for each of us.

Beloved of God, Jesus has written a special delivery letter, certified by God and delivered by the Holy Spirit. The letter is not a chain letter, not a forwarded e-mail, not a Dear John or Jane letter, and not a photocopied letter. This letter is to be given to each person who is willing to follow the new commandment. It is personally addressed with names that only God knows. It is sent with love to all who would take the bread and the cup and remember Jesus' sacrifice for us.

Dear Friends, My Brothers and My Sisters,
Heirs to the Kingdom:

I pray this letter finds you well. I know that Satan is busy trying to sift you like wheat. I know that the road has been a little rough and your going has been a little tough. I realize that there have been mountains and valleys in your life. Sometimes you wanted to give up. The tunnel seemed too dark, and the pain was too great. Please know that I am aware of all your trials and successes. If you will allow me, let me begin by telling you how proud I am of you. I know that the easy way would have been to just join the other side, but you have held on and held out. I may not be there with you the way I was with my disciples in that upper room at the Last Supper, but I am with you always. I am in the wind that cools you in the heat of the day, I am in the water that cleanses you. I am with you even in those pains you have as the days go by and the seasons of your life change.

I continue to give you a spiritual transfusion when it seems as if you cannot go on with life. I am there when you are disappointed and when you are overjoyed. I am writing now to let you know how much I love you because you have remembered me. I have tried to send a message before, but you were a little preoccupied. I tried to write through the garden, the flood, the exodus, the prophets, and even a short tenure on earth. I tried to write to you in ink—even cyberspace—but the connection seemed too slow or the system timed out. But tonight I am writing in blood, so you can contemplate the brilliance of the crimson, burgundy, fuchsia, and red against the backdrop of the purple of my royalty and divinity. I need you to understand that our relationship is one-on-one. Nothing and no one can come between us. I love you equally with your brothers and sisters. This is a love letter written in blood just for you.

How do I love you? Let me count the ways. I love you to the depth, breadth, and height my soul can reach. I will and do love you more after my death and resurrection. I love you from heaven. I love you in your soul. I love you so much I am coming back to get you when God gives me the signal. How do I love you? Let me count the ways. I love you with:

1. Atonement—I made the sacrifice to unite you with God's love.
2. Benevolence—I provide companionship while you are still turning from sin.
3. Compassion—When you are in spiritual distress, I come to ease your pain.
4. Divinity—I am God's only begotten Son; I was there in the beginning and will be with you in the end.
5. Equality—I am no respector of persons; all are equal in my sight.
6. Faithfulness—I will do just what I promised.
7. Grace—unmerited favor. I look beyond your faults and see your needs.
8. Hope—You may be going through a lot now, but I already have your escape plan in place.
9. Intercession—I advocate for you daily; I stand in the gap for you.
10. Justice—I weigh the evidence and decide your fate.

How do I love you? Let me count the ways. I love you with:

11. King—all power in heaven and earth is in my hands.
12. Life—you were dead in your sins, and I died for you.
13. Miracles—I can make all things brand new.
14. Newness—I will take away your old thoughts, old relationships, old ways.
15. Omni—I am omnipotent, omniscient, and omnipresent.
16. Peace—I am the calm in the midst of your storms.
17. Quiet—in the rushing of your days I am the silence you need for reflection.
18. Redemption—I paid the price for your liberty.
19. Salvation—I snatched you from certain death.
20. Truth—I cannot lie.

How do I love you? Let me count the ways. I love you with:

21. Unction—I am the anointing that destroys all yokes.
22. Victory—I overcame hell, death, and the grave so you would know that you can conquer all things.
23. Wisdom—I know your thoughts before you form them and your needs before you ask.
24. Excellence—I am the name above all names. At the sound of my name every knee shall bow and every tongue confess me as Savior and Lord.
25. Yearning—I want you to be with me in that New Jerusalem.
26. Zeal—I go out of my way to rescue you. I am passionate about your receipt of eternal life.

I love you in all these ways and in more ways than you can ever comprehend. Whatever happens in your life, remember these words. Remember this letter. Remember me. I have to go now, but know that I am only a prayer away. Just keep remembering that I love you. As you eat the bread and take the cup, remember to love others just as I have loved and do love you. It will be worth it all when I come back. See you soon.

Love, Your Friend,
Jesus

My sisters and my brothers. Have you read your letter today? Have you taken the information from your letter and stored it in that special delivery place deep down inside that only you and God know about? Have you hidden God's Word in your heart? Can we live in love through the blood of Jesus? The mothers and fathers knew about love letters written in blood. They survived so they could pass the love down to us. They ask the same questions we can ask tonight as we prepare to feast together as Jesus commanded. What can wash away my sins? Nothing but the blood of Jesus. Amen.

CHAPTER 3

Jana Childers

Sometimes I think it might have been better if nobody had ever told me how long preparing a sermon is supposed to take. But twenty-some years ago somebody did tell me about the "one hour in study for every minute in the pulpit" rule. I am sorry to say that not only did it prove true in my experience, but every year now I hand it on as advice to my students. I hope I am not doing them a disservice. It does take me a long time to bring a sermon into this world. So far it has seemed better to be honest about that.

Certainly it does not seem as if it should take twenty hours to get ready for the moments that comprise a mere 25 percent of the worship service, but week after week, somehow it does. Although I've preached many sermons that cost me more hours than they were supposed to, I have never preached one that cost me less. I comfort myself by repeating the passage from the end of 2 Samuel, "I will not serve God with that which costs me nothing."[1] But it is not always satisfying. Not only do David's words ring a bit false in my mouth, I am often left wondering how much of my stressing and straining is valuable to God and how much is my own neurotic wheel-spinning.

Preaching costs me plenty—let me just say that right up front. Mostly it costs time and adrenaline, but it also exacts prices that are not so obvious. Preaching makes me very anxious. It also makes me euphoric and deeply gratified, but those are points for another section of this essay. I think it's only fair to start by talking about the strain that accompanies the process. Although stress seems to play a larger role in some preachers' creative work than others, no good preacher completely avoids anxious moments. For many of us, anxiety is not only an inescapable part of preaching, it is a necessary component.

I count myself among the preachers and other artists whose process seems to work by way of "friction" or "spark." Philosophers such as Samuel Coleridge who describe creativity as a product of opposites[2] have helped me understand something about my own process. Out of the friction between two juxtaposed ideas, a spark is born. Insight, clarity, and imaginative leaps are the result. This, of course, may be little comfort to the preacher who is not sure she is going to be able to hold her stomach contents in place during the process. However, for some of us, creativity seems to *have* to work this way. For us, anxiety is a catalyst, setting one concept at odds with another. It fuels conflict—at least within the preacher and often within the sermon. For me, a sermon is born out of the conflict of two ideas.

"A Shameless Path," the sermon that appears at the end of this chapter, provides an example of one of the most obvious kinds of conflict, the "how could Jesus (or the Bible) say this?" kind. It confronts the saying "Ask and it shall be given you" head on. It is a sermon born of a wrestling match. In the initial stages of preparation, I was not so much "struggling with the text" as I was attacking it outright. I was wrestling *against* it. "Come on, you can't get away with that!" I told Luke over and over again, playing the arguments out in my head. (It is so much easier to have imaginary debates with an evangelist than with a Savior. It's a good thing for me that Jesus didn't write his own gospel.) All the while, of course, I was wrestling against my own anxiety, letting the flames from one fire lick the other until the two swirled together and—eventually—burned down to a nice bank of coals.

When the creative process works this way, there is nothing like it. When it doesn't, an understanding of the process can at least help diagnose the trouble. One way I know that my process can be described in terms of the "spark" model of creativity is that it is the theory that best explains my failures. When one of my sermons goes wrong, it is almost always because (a) there were too many ideas vying with each other, (b) I couldn't decide which of them the sermon was really about, and/or (c) the conflicting ideas never really did come to resolution. Occasionally, I have trouble with conflicting ideas that turn out not to have enough fizz in them—where what seems at first like juicy conflict turns out to be only a small semantic problem or an issue that has no practical ramifications. But usually, when I write a sermon that just will not line up—whose ideas will not toe the line or flow or proceed logically from one to another—it is because my anxiety has overwhelmed my creative process instead of fueling it. When that happens, I end up with homiletical mud, several vying ideas that have beat each other bloody trying to play off each other. But when it works, when the ideas bounce and coalesce and resolve, the sermon flies. For me, so far, the ecstasy of homiletical flight has always been worth the cost. Of course, that doesn't keep me from worrying.

Over the years of worrying about worrying, I have learned a few things that help me avoid the homiletical mud. What follows are my personal tips for persuading anxiety and creativity to shake hands. Some of them are peculiar to me. Some of them are universal. Most of them are more applicable to preachers who struggle than to those who find preaching to be a felicitous task. Not everybody is an anxious preacher. If you are, I hope some of these will work for you.

Be honest with yourself about how long it takes. For years I fervently hoped that after I found my voice and my feet as a preacher, had preached two or three hundred sermons, and achieved spiritual maturity, my sermons would fall together in, say, ten hours instead of twenty. Every time I wrote a new sermon, I would start the week thinking, "This might be the breakthrough point!" By the time I realized that it wasn't going to be, I had used up all of what was supposed to have been my day off and was over-tired as well as discouraged. I am in my third decade as a preacher now, and though I have seen the shrinking workweek miracle happen to some of my friends, it has yet to happen to me. It takes me three or four two-hour blocks and two or three four-hour blocks to write a sermon.

Remember this: "Writers require solitude." I found it very freeing to hear a writing teacher say this straight out. There is nothing wrong with you if you can't compose your sermons and supervise your children's homework at the same time. Writers require solitude. So do preachers who compose orally or use notes. Not only does preaching take most of us a significant amount of time, it takes alone-time. One of the leading creativity theorists of the twentieth century, University of Chicago's Mihaly Csikszentmihalyi, believes that the ability to tolerate time alone is one of the key characteristics of creative people.

> Most people cannot put up with solitude for very long. After a few minutes, and certainly after a few hours, they start to feel a kind of psychic entropy. They are unable to coordinate their thoughts…to keep from feeling unhappy or bored, they pick up a telephone or turn on the television.[3]

Like most preachers I know, I require at least one long stretch of time to simmer, untangle, and elaborate on the sermon's main ideas, "psychic entropy" or not! It is even better for the sermon when I can get three or four. Let me hasten to say that this is not always time I relish. As Csikszentmihalyi suggests, solitude can make a person crazy. I am not an outrageous introvert. On the Myers-Briggs personality inventory, I consistently test in the middle of the introversion/extroversion scale ("Never happy," my husband says. "Well-adjusted," I claim). Tolerating more and longer periods of solitude is something that I have learned to do.

It is possible to train the unconscious to kick in. I had a mentor who, week after week through all the years of his preaching ministry, kept a ten o'clock appointment with the Holy Spirit every Tuesday morning. He told me not long before he died last year at the age of eighty-four that he had never been stood up. Every sermon he had ever preached had started in one of those appointments. From him I learned that it is helpful to have a routine for creative tasks, not so much for the Holy Spirit's benefit as for mine!

It is not surprising, when you stop to think about it, that the mind and heart need a certain amount of conditioning to do creative work. Why should the creative task be different from any other discipline? Artists have always known that if you want to access the unconscious, the seat of creative, associative thought, it is necessary to cultivate a relationship with it. Some find that set times, regular "appointments," and rituals help. In her very funny book on creative process, *Bird by Bird*, Anne Lamott advocates sitting down to write at the same time every day.[4] The writer's guru Julia Cameron requires her students to start every morning writing three longhand pages.[5] For generations, acting teachers have been recommending yoga and other similar physical disciplines as aids in "stilling" the conscious mind and accessing the unconscious. I find all these tools useful, not as substitutes for divine inspiration but as forms of prayer, which help open me to cooperation with the Holy Spirit.

Repetitive large muscle movement can help you overcome writer's block. Physical activity—especially rhythmic movement that involves large muscle groups—does two things that are strategically important to a game plan: It dissipates anxiety and quiets the conscious mind. In one fell swoop you not only do what you can to control the adrenaline your body is hyper-secreting, you achieve an optimal state of mind for the creative task. It's not for no reason that many of the great preachers of the ages were pacers. Some contemporary preachers may prefer jogging, raking, or even vacuuming to old-fashioned pacing, but any rhythmic movement will do. Like many preachers, I find that my brain serves up that elusive sentence more often in the shower or the car than at my desk.

I depend on my muscles to do a big part of my thinking. Giving my voice and body to the text—reading the biblical text out loud, pacing while reading, and projecting myself into the biblical author's shoes—often tells me as much about a text as the commentators do. Out-loud performance—of the biblical text and of the sermon manuscript as it develops—is the most valuable tool I have.

Expect distracting thoughts. They're a normal part of the process. What could be more natural than that when you sit down to write the sermon, errands and household chores crowd your mind? It only shows that your brain is engaged. The gears are turning. Sorting and remembering are two of the brain's favorite functions, and by "sitting down to do some serious work," you have just called them up. It is not their fault that you have more files stored in the mental computer than the ones concerned with sermon writing. It is nobody's fault, in fact. They are just doing the job you have asked them to do, starting on a (personal) global scale. Eventually they will focus down to the specific task at hand, but fighting them during their "warm up" period won't get you there any faster.

Instead of eating up creative energy with guilt about chores left undone or with annoyance at myself ("Where are my powers of concentration?!"), it has helped me to realize that it is *normal* for a person's brain to begin the creative process this way and that the part of the process in which chores keep popping into my mind won't last long. Placing a separate pad alongside my sermon notes has also been useful. That way, when a mental image of heaped-up laundry pops into my mind, I just write "laundry" on the pad and return to my notes. Often the act of writing the word down is enough to relieve the compulsion. I don't actually have to get up, go to the basement, and load the washer. On the occasions when writing the word on the pad still leaves me antsy, I can usually tell myself that I will reward forty-five (or sixty) minutes' work with a break that will include a trip to the basement and, perhaps, an Oreo.

Daily faithfulness is more important than sacrifice. A few years ago, I started out to preach a series and ended up at a revival. Who knew that the lovely group of mainline Protestants who had shown up at the conference grounds that summer would be interested in such a thing? I couldn't have been more surprised. What an exciting thing for a preacher! As soon as I began to see the signs of what was happening, I redoubled my prayer life. By the third day of the week, I was waking early to walk out to the outdoor prayer chapel by the lake and beseech God to use the power of my preaching to change lives. I laid siege to the gates of heaven, "humbled" myself before God, searched my heart, interceded for the nice folks, even shed a few tears. I begged God to guide my preaching, to inspire the listeners, to speak through me, to speak to me. And I got a reply. I got, in fact, a very clear reply. One of the clearer "voices" I have ever heard God use said, "Quit trying to storm the throne." Then, more faintly, "It is daily faithfulness I desire."

Daily faithfulness is not something that I have ever been good at. In the early years of my ministry, I depended on crisis to fuel my sermons. It was the way I managed my anxiety. Before I sat down to write the sermon, I would let the busyness of the week build up a head of steam. Only at the last possible moment, after I had answered every urgent and semi-urgent pastoral need the congregation had, would I begin serious work on the sermon. I was one of those preachers who had to paint myself into a situational corner to force myself to write. It took a lot of external pressure ("you're really out of time now!") to overcome my internal resistance to facing the blank page. In fact, it took more every week.

You would think I might have learned the lesson quickly, but it's amazing how many crises a young preacher can take. Eventually, of course, middle age catches up to all of us. Sure enough, right on schedule with my middle years has come an increased appreciation for routines. Now my process has more to do with keeping quote notebooks, maintaining a devotional life, and making room for regular conversations with colleagues than it used to. I try to leave myself time to collaborate,[6] to "soak" in ideas and images, and to walk. Of all the changes, adding a significant amount of walking to my life was the most radical. It is also the one I manage to be most consistent about. Little wonder that the dominant metaphor running through the last few years' worth of my sermons has been The Path.

The Holy Spirit needs an editor. Ann and Barry Ulanov make the same point more gracefully in *Primary Speech,* their book on prayer. "The spirit moves in simultaneities," they explain:

> Where we demand some reasonable association of ideas, or even of emotions, looking almost always for antecedents to explain consequences, the spirit gathers everything up at once and deposits it in one massive offering to our understanding. We are, all of us, creatures of parts, used to beginnings, middles, and ends because our lives are divided that way, and our language and our way of talking in language follows the same logic of process. But the spirit is one and undivided.[7]

The Ulanovs' observation goes a long way toward explaining why, in more than fifteen years of full-time teaching, I have never met a beginning preacher who could write a strong sermon by taking dictation from the Holy Spirit. I have met many who thought they could or should, but their sermons are invariably incoherent. Why? The Spirit is not big on sequential movement. Segues, transitions, linear flow, and homiletical form are the preacher's job, not the Paraclete's. For most preachers, divine inspiration comes, when it comes, in the shape of images, phrases, and ideas that still need to be put in some kind of order.

Unfortunately, putting ideas and images in order is pretty much the hardest part of the preaching task. Any person of faith can stand up and say something that is true. Many can even do a respectable job of interpreting a biblical text. However, to integrate several ideas into a clear and compelling whole can be very hard work. In my case, I would die happy if I could just learn to tell the rabbit trails from the main road. Chasing red herrings and putting too much stock in flashes of promising ideas are two of my biggest downfalls. I am trying to learn to let go of ideas, to come more quickly to the realization that idea "x" or image "y" really belongs in sermon about "z" and not in the sermon on "q" that is on my desk at the moment.

Sometimes, in order to get a particularly persistent thought off the desk, it helps to write it out and file it. That way, I can say to myself, "It will be there when I need it next week." Interestingly enough, the sermon pieces that have accumulated in my drawer over the years turn out to have a couple of things in common. They all tend to be stories I felt especially passionate about when they first occurred to me. A lot of them are about my grandmother. Some of them are subtly self-congratulatory. Most of them, once they are placed in the drawer, never again see the light of day.

It is more important to say something timely than something original. It took me a long time to realize that God was not expecting a fresh, new insight every time I preached. After I had been preaching for a few years, it occurred to me that God might not ever be expecting one. Because of this little vanity of mine, though, I used to have a great deal of trouble telling people what my theme sentence was. They all sounded so pedestrian. How could I admit that my sermon could be boiled down to "God is quicker to hear than we are to ask" or "Prayer is a good thing"? Wasn't that tantamount to admitting that I was about to preach pabulum, old-hat chestnuts, or clichés? Who would want to show up on Sunday if I admitted to them during the week ahead that I was planning on preaching on the theme "God is very, very big"?

It was pride that led me into the slough of obfuscation and vanity that kept me there. Eventually, I was delivered by the feedback of a very gracious congregation. What worked for them, they lovingly let me know, was a theme that connected to the conversations they'd been having in their kitchens and bedrooms that week. They didn't need me to invent new spiritual gadgets for them; they needed to hear the connection made between their worlds and God's. Now I tell my students that theme sentences should sound as if you're speaking to kindergartners. The purpose of a theme sentence is to help you keep your focus, not to advertise the erudition of your sermon. I also tell them that it is important to listen to what your congregation asks for. A good congregation is the best homiletics professor a preacher can have.

Find out where your best starting point is. I know some people who start their sermons at the end. I know plenty who always work from an outline and others who build a sermon around a key story. Many seem to do well by starting with a general idea of what the body of the sermon is going to be. For me, it is important to feel that the opening is right.

My sermons are more likely to develop out of an opening image, vignette, quote, or question than any other way. I write as they say novelists write, letting the sermon lead me from thought to thought and only discovering two-thirds of the way through the "answer" to the "question" I've been pursuing. Although I find the idea of intentionally writing rough drafts attractive, it never really works for me. Though I end up with many drafts, I seem to have to believe that the one I'm working on at the moment is "it." I hone the rhythm, word choice, and syntax of each sentence as I go. It almost seems as if a "defective" sentence is enough to trip me up; the flow of the process stops until I satisfy myself (though often only temporarily) that the wrinkle is ironed out.

Using this method means that there is a great deal of pressure on the first sentence. Some of that pressure is legitimate, I think, because the opening sentence is so important. It gives the preacher her best chance to grab the congregation—a chance she will never have in the same way again throughout the rest of the sermon. I am always amazed at preachers who casually throw away the golden moment with "When I was thinking about today's text yesterday, it occurred to me that…" or even "Well, I don't really like today's text very much." Although I don't always find a blockbuster sentence for the opening of the sermon, I always try. I try to honor the opportunity that moment represents.

Using the novelist's method of writing also means that the title is the last thing I know about a sermon. When I was in parish ministry, the person who was typing the bulletin was on the other side of the wall from the person who was writing the sermon. Somehow, this meant that we were often able to negotiate an eleventh-hour change, so that what the congregation saw in the bulletin was at least an in-the-ballpark title, if not the best title. However, these days I preach as a guest in someone else's pulpit, and titles are once again an issue for me. This means that though I turn the necessary information in to the church office on the required day, most congregations I preach to now never get to know the sermon's *real* title. This bothered me a bit at first, but eventually it dawned on me that a title rarely has anything to do with the success or failure of a sermon. In fact, it seems to me that the most powerful thing about titles is the power you give them to hem you in.

Permit yourself a vice. I have three bad habits without which I could not preach. I try not to indulge in more than one per sermon, but when it comes to managing the creative process, I find that there is nothing as comforting as a small guilty pleasure. It will be up to you to find those that work best for you, given the uniqueness of your tastes and the contours of your own psyche. When the realm of God is fully arrived, of course, none of us will need crutches, rewards, comforts—or even books of advice—to get us through the birth of a sermon. However, for now…I believe God understands.

The sermon that follows is one I have preached in several different forms. I have a ten-minute version, a seventeen-minute version, and a twenty-five minute version of this sermon in my files. The version I've included here is my favorite and the one I consider the "most finished." Both of the fine scholars who were teaching New Testament studies at San Francisco Theological Seminary at the time I wrote the sermon were instrumental in helping me wrestle Luke to the ground. Herman Waetjen and Antoinette Clark Wire are generous and brilliant colleagues. Without their help, my notes on Luke 11 would still be sitting (along with my notes on Mark 8) in the file in my bottom drawer marked "Impossible Texts."

A Shameless Path

LUKE 11:1–13

"Nearer than hands and feet": That's what God is when we pray. "Speak to him for he heareth and spirit with spirit can meet. Closer is he than breathing, nearer than hands and feet." Alfred Lord Tennyson.[8] The poets have a high view of prayer, some of them anyway. The mere mention of the subject seems to send them running for the card file marked "sublimity," where they pull out adjectives— sweet hours, precious moments, privileged meetings. Before you know it, the violins are swelling and we're wending our way through a dewy rose garden, walking and talking with a certain Someone whose voice, as one gospel songwriter put it, is "so sweet the birds hush their singing."[9] Prayer to a poet—or a gospel songwriter—is like romance to Barry Manilow: an irresistible topic.

I don't know about you, but as much as I love the poets and especially the gospel songwriters, and as much as I want to know the nearer-than-hands-or-feet God, I have to say it: My prayer life is not much like a walk through a rose garden. Not only does Jesus not come to the garden alone to see me, not walk with me and talk with me, not meet me in the garden, lots of times I wonder if I'm even in the right zip code. My prayer life is not much like a dewy garden path. And that's why I come to today's scripture lesson with high hopes.

After all, I believe—I think many of us instinctively believe— that there is something to this thing called prayer. We know about what happens in foxholes. We pay attention when a person we admire says she will pray for us. We see prayer working in other people's lives. And we believe Mother Teresa—don't we?—when she says, "No prayer, no faith; no faith, no love; no love, no devotion; no devotion, no service." "Yes," we say, "I need that in my life!" For once we are right there in the front row of the classroom with the disciples, waving our hands and saying, "Lord! Teach me how to do this!"

45

And Jesus says, in the translation of New Testament scholar Antoinette Clark Wire, "Everyone who asks receives. The one who seeks, finds. And the one who knocks, gets in the door."[10] The Gospel according to Luke is not easy to hear today, not easy to preach, because it is not easy to believe. "Ask and it shall be given you?!" How could Jesus have said such a thing? How could that be true?

If it were true, of course, all the eight-year-old girls in the world would be braiding pink satin ribbons into the tails of their very own ponies. If it were true, all the eight-year-old girls in the world and their brothers and sisters would go to bed every night with just the right blend of fats and carbohydrates and proteins in their blood streams. If it were true, all the children of the world would at the least—at the very least—be living in peace. "Ask and it shall be given you" is an outrageous thing, perhaps even an obscene thing to say to a world whose decade in review pictures are going to include Bosnia, Rwanda, Iraq, Oklahoma City. How could Jesus say such a thing?

"Oh well," we say, "maybe this is just meant for the ears of the disciples. Maybe Jesus was making that promise to those who are, you know, the spiritual elite." I have to say I don't think you can interpret the text that way, since, in Luke, the disciples are pictured as anything but elite. "Okay," we say, "maybe Jesus means that *eventually,* out at the end of time, you will get what you ask for." But that's not a very convincing argument either, especially since Jesus goes right on from making the ask-and-receive promise to comparing the whole thing to hungry children asking their parents for food...not an "eventually" kind of thing! "All right," we say, "maybe it means that if we ask in accordance with God's will, then we will see our prayers answered." And maybe that is true. But I don't see how that helps explain this particular text, because there is no such qualifier in the immediate or larger context of this passage.

Okay, then, how could Jesus say such a thing?

The first thing we notice when we look closely at what Jesus said was that he did not say, "Ask and you will get what you ask for." What he said was something more like, "Ask and you will get something good." Notice the syntax of the rhetorical question he asks after he makes the great promise: "If your children ask for fish, will you give them a snake?" Do you see how that's not the same thing as saying, "If they ask for fish, don't you give them fish?" Even

Jesus' word choice makes it clear that the promise he's making is not as tit-for-tat as the promise we want to hear.

The second thing we notice is that there is something lost in the translation of the New Testament Greek into English here. The Greek does not say, "Ask and you will receive." It says "Aaaaaask and keep on asking…Seeeeeek and keep on seeking…Knoooock and keep on knocking." The Greek verb implies ongoing action. Be persistent, Jesus is saying. Be shameless. Run right up to that door and pound on it. Make a fool out of yourself with your asking.

Finally, the thing that is most often overlooked about the story Jesus tells here is that this is primarily a story about intercessory prayer.[11] One friend goes to another friend on behalf of someone else. This is not a story about little girls praying to get a handsome husband when they grow up. This is not a story about young adults who beseech God for help in getting the right job. This is not even about older believers who bring their legitimate prayer concerns about their own health before God. This is primarily a story about intercessory prayer.

It is this kind of prayer—shameless, persistent, intercessory prayer—that Jesus guarantees.

I hope you have known a prayer warrior. I have. When she died some years ago, at the age of eighty-eight, I took the plaque that had hung in her house for more than sixty years and hung it in mine. It says, "Prayer Changes Things." I fussed and puttered for a while over the question of where to hang it. The front hall seemed so public. The dining room? Too preachy. The den? Well, it looked quite out of place over the big screen TV.

I wondered what the people who visit my house would think. Such an old-fashioned thought. The words are not even attributable to a respectable theologian. Ultimately, I hung the plaque in my old-fashioned kitchen. I do see people eyeing it sometimes as they chat to me before a dinner party. And I do wonder what they think. Maybe if they know it was my grandmother's, they think I'm sentimental. And I am. Maybe if they know me well, they think I need help to keep on believing those words. And I do.

It's not easy to believe. It's not easy to *keep on* believing in prayer. But if you've known the kind of prayer warriors I have, you have to stay at the table with the question. Because beyond coincidence and synchronicity, beyond luck and happenstance, there is something that Jesus was pointing to and that prayer warriors know, something that changes people if not things. Something our grandmothers called "answered prayer." On my own grandmother's list there were lots of them: the alcoholic son who finds his way home against all odds, the troubled community able to mend its fences despite the things that were said, the word of forgiveness that comes at the last possible moment.

"What is the secret to answered prayer?" the disciples asked Jesus. "What is the secret to answered prayer?" "Asking." Little by little and here and there and now and then, the kingdom of God is breaking in through the efforts of those who ask.

Oh yes, in the lives of all the prayer warriors I have known there are unanswered prayers and prayers that stay on the list for decades. There are seasons of doubt, sometimes even public failure. But there is not much of one thing. There is not much shame. Not much spiritual shyness. There is instead a gung-ho-ness, a readiness to ask, a willingness to throw themselves headlong into a situation of need— to jump off the porch and take off running across the back yard, skirts flying and apron flapping, through the fence and up the steps to that oh-so familiar door. There is a willingness to beat a path, to beat a shameless path, to God's door…in the asking, the prayer warriors say, is the secret.

Last year, I set my foot on an ugly path, a path not entirely my own. I was keeping company with my friend Lucy as she followed out the last twelve months of her life. During those months I learned what many of you who have walked with cancer already know— what a privilege it can be to join your prayers with those of a woman of faith who is facing her death. Time and again last Spring, Lucy urged me to accompany her to heaven's door, as she rang its bells, rattled its gates, and slammed its knockers, not on her own behalf, but for those she would leave behind. We prayed for her husband, her little girl, her mother, and her father. We prayed. Some of us for lack of anything better to do. Some of us out of hearts full of faith. Some of us because we believed Lucy when she said she could feel our prayers. She was buoyed by them, she said, reminding us of what Charles Williams called the intercessory prayers of believers—"the glorious web." We did form a kind of a web with our prayers. Me praying for Lucy in Atlanta from my home in California, Ron from Indianapolis, Gene from Kansas City, Pam from Toronto, and countless others.

In the last few months of her earthly life, Lucy's own prayers were filled with a deep sense of God's presence. It often came to her wrapped in the words and music of a hymn. She came out of surgery one time with the words rolling up through her—"The Lone, Wild Bird" one time, and "Jesu, Joy of Man's Desiring" another. Toward the end, she told me, it was the gospel songs that sustained her. As they welled up in her, she gathered visitors around her bed to sing them. This web of song and prayer sustained Lucy until that morning in July when her feet were lifted off the path and she was ushered through the door. The word of Lucy's death went out quickly over the well-established grapevine, and by the time the hearse came to take her body, fifty-five friends had gathered. They flanked the walk and filled the porches of the little house, and they sang the body out. They sang "I'll Fly Away."

In the lives of all the prayer warriors I have known, there is heartbreak and loss, but there is not much despair. There is instead an invisible web that buoys them up and, ultimately, carries them home. What did Lucy get for all her praying? Did she get remission? Did she avoid pain? Did she see an angel? No. What Lucy got is what we all get. She got God, the God who is nearer than hands and feet.

God's own presence is the answer to every prayer, the answer that surpasses anything we could ask for. Ask, Jesus says, and it shall be given you.

CHAPTER 4

Linda L. *Clader*

It certainly doesn't always go easily. There are plenty of times when I run late, and try to squeeze my whole preparation into an inadequate space, and wind up staring at an accusing, blank screen, the only person left awake in a darkened house. But this time things went the way they sometimes do, when I feel as if I am more an observer than the composer of the sermon. I believe there were several reasons it went so smoothly: I was blessed with an exceptional consultant who was both a friend and an inspiration to keep my process "singing"; I was preaching from a text that resonated easily and colorfully with my own experience and that of my congregation; and I just happened to have witnessed something recently that offered me the catalyst I needed to focus my sermon. I offer it to you not necessarily as a typical outcome of a typical preparation, but as the outcome of one time when my process actually followed the pattern that I believe in.

I was scheduled to preach at a week-long workshop for seminarians called the "Preaching Excellence Program," supported and directed by the Episcopal Preaching Foundation. This was a workshop for which I had taught a number of times before, so although I did not know the specific people who would be in the congregation, I did have a general picture. I also knew that I would be preaching and presiding at the eucharist on the first morning of the regular week of workshops. That is, about an hour after the service, the first students would be preaching a homily before their peers from other seminaries.

Does it go without saying that such a congregation is an anxious group? Do I need to mention that there is just the tiniest bit of competition among our Episcopal seminaries? Although for the most part our students (and faculty) treat one another respectfully, should I perhaps point out that there are a few differences of theological position in the Episcopal church, and that they often surface when students from different seminaries try to preach to one another? As I began to think about the sermon to come, these were the dimensions of the occasion that were uppermost in my mind. The people in that congregation would all be anxious. The students would feel on the spot among peers they did not yet know. Ditto, of course, the teachers. There would be a lot of electricity in the room—mental and emotional and spiritual static. My task would be to channel the electricity into a useful form of energy and to cooperate with the eucharistic celebration in renewing everyone's faith in grace over prowess.

All that was a given before I even glanced at the texts for the day. When I did, I knew that I had been offered a gift. The liturgical environment for the sermon would be the church's commemoration of Mary's visit to her cousin Elizabeth, the Feast of the Visitation—what we Episcopalians call a "red-letter day." In the context of the week of workshops, having a red-letter day to work with meant we could pull out all the liturgical stops, and no one could accuse us of going overboard. The service would be sung; the organ prelude and postlude would be big; the mood would be joyful. The feast was dictated by our liturgical calendar, and so only by chance did it fall on the first day of the conference. But it was perfect. All that nervous energy could potentially be converted into enthusiastic music-making. *And…* it was a Marian festival, a commemoration of a meeting between women.

Besides the sermon itself, my responsibility included planning the liturgy for that day, which is not an unusual situation for a preacher. What made it unusual for me, however, was that I was doing it in close collaboration with an exceptional musician and liturgist, my close friend and former colleague Dr. Alan Lewis. Alan and I had planned many liturgical events together over the years for worship at our seminary, and we operated on the same wavelength. So by e-mail and over the phone, we shared our creative impulses. I requested Alan's ideas for music. He sent some and then requested ideas about my sermon. I sent the sermon by e-mail and asked for response and criticism. Alan responded and adjusted the music.

We consulted on which liturgical forms to use. Because this feast day and my sermon centered on two women, we wanted to be careful to make all the language gender-inclusive; but because this would be the first liturgy of the week of workshops, neither did we want it to be shocking. We looked at the "alternative" liturgies produced by our national church and chose one that had imagery in the Eucharistic Prayer about giving birth. Alan wrote and I edited the intercessory prayers based on the language and imagery of the Song of Mary from the Gospel lesson. We chose a concluding blessing that continued the image of God as Mother.

I have described this part of my process in some detail because, ideally, all the components I mentioned above do participate in my sermon planning. In the Episcopal Church, the readings for a Sunday or feast day are a given. But even when I am "guest-preaching" somewhere, I always try to find out what music has been chosen for the liturgy; and when I am in "home-territory," I often make suggestions as my sermon begins to take shape. Ideally, the person who is leading the intercessory prayers will also be consulting with me about ideas and themes that should appear again in that portion of the liturgy. My intent is that the liturgy of the word and the liturgy of the table should echo and complement each other, so that those who worship together on that occasion will experience the event as an integrated whole.

My process in planning the sermon itself, as a result, often takes a spiral shape. It is impossible to say which I think about first— occasion, congregation, or text. The congregations among whom I most often preach swim around in my subconscious all the time, so it would be laughable to try and pinpoint a moment in the process when I let them into my composing. As I gain comfort with biblical materials, the same is happening there. And the occasion itself keeps evolving: I may know at the beginning of a week that I will be preaching on the tenth Sunday in Pentecost, but only late in the week will I know that the church leaders have voted to build the access ramp into the church building, or that the secretary's mother just died, or that there has been a world event that must be addressed. So I take a step forward and then revisit all the information about context I have already received. And always I am returning to the place of the sermon in the worship event—music, prayers, color, choreography, the sending-forth of the faithful at the end of it all.

Because I believe so fiercely that preaching is part of an integrated worship event, I try as I am musing to keep relating the texts for the day to the eucharist, to prayer. I do a good deal of this unconsciously, because I have been an Episcopalian all my life and my grasp of what worship or preaching means has been formed by my experience worshiping in community. But I also do it intentionally, trying as often as I can to pause in my process of sermon preparation and pray.

I am no spiritual giant. I have had some short spells in my life when I was able to sit quietly and meditate for twenty minutes at a time, but that is not my pattern today. My prayer life today is much more a running conversation between me and God. When something that concerns me enters into my consciousness, I'll sort of kiss it and send it along to God. The words are few and the visual images many. The metaphor for God that is working best for me right now is something like holy breath, really Spirit in the basic sense of the word. That's where I am as I write this essay; tomorrow I could be somewhere else entirely.

When I begin my focused work on a sermon, I often read the texts with prayer beforehand. I ask God to open my ears and heart to receive the Word, and I ask for guidance from the Holy Spirit so that I can proclaim what God's people need to hear. I do it about as simply as I just wrote it, and then I read the texts. On the first day of my preparation, that is all I do. I might read them more than once. Sometimes, rarely, I actually read them out loud, but because I am a classicist by training, I tend to read everything with my ears anyway, even when my lips don't move. In any event, I believe that hearing the readings is important, partly because that is how the congregation will encounter the text, and partly because I know that the Holy Spirit gains access to me through all my senses, and I need to open as many doors as possible for that to happen.

Throughout the week, I return to the texts in this simple way. I am undisciplined about these returns—I keep the Bible open and marked next to my computer, so when I am getting my e-mail I am also glancing back at the coming readings. I have a load of Bible software on the computer, so at some point early in the week I start poking around in commentaries and other translations to see what I can see, hear what I can hear. My computer sits below four shelves of various other exegetical resources, and from time to time I notice a book on the shelf and I pull it down and sniff around. Sometime early in the week, I will spend an hour or two in the (to me) very pleasurable task of intense exegesis.

My exegetical process always includes several phases, not necessarily in any given order. Because I am trained as a classicist, I am facile with New Testament Greek, and I easily get lured into treasure hunts for the meaning and usage of Greek expressions. I almost always consult Malina and Rohrbaugh's social-science commentaries on the gospels,[1] and whenever the text I am investigating has also been investigated by Raymond Brown, I plunge into his commentaries with relish.[2] Because I do not have much facility with Hebrew, I am more dependent—and more limited—in my use of Old Testament commentaries. This is my historical-critical phase.

I am also devoted to the idea of taking seriously the narrative as it is presented in the text at hand, and I have been helped by numerous books on reading scripture as narrative. Most of these provide what I would term "deep exegesis," or general background that shapes my hermeneutical stance toward the text. The gospel of Luke, from which the sermon below emerged, lends itself well to this approach, particularly because of the rich two-volume story presented in the gospel and Acts.[3] But I have spent a lifetime teaching literature, and that has deeply influenced the way I read scripture. So when I think about biblical narrative, I am also hearing echoes of Homer's *Odyssey* and various Greek dramas, as well as a few favorite films that take an interesting approach to storytelling.[4]

Our lectionary often connects the gospel text with the Old Testament reading in a typological fashion. So I usually spend some time thinking about how the two readings echo each other or how one might illuminate the story or thematic material of the other. I look at the psalm and the epistle for the day and make notes on imagery or themes that resonate in the other readings (I often do this in the context of choosing hymns for the occasion). I almost never focus my preaching on anything but the Old Testament text or the gospel.

Those are the more scholarly phases of my exegetical process. Because I have struggled all my life to keep my devotion to learning from getting dusty, I insist that this part of my preparation is "spiritual." I can encounter the Holy Spirit just as immediately through my pleasure trolling the depths of a Greek lexicon as I do when I am bowed in silent prayer. But the language, the mode of conversation, is different.

As I explore the dictionaries and read and reread the scriptural texts themselves, I also take note of the way the stories connect with my senses. Sometimes I'm conscious about this aspect of exegesis, and sometimes not. But it's a way of engaging the text in an embodied as well as an intellectual way. I imagine being one or another of the characters in the story. I imagine being an onlooker, or someone who is just hearing about an event. I consciously steer away from identifying with Jesus. I look around at the countryside or the room where the action takes place. I feel the warmth of the sun, smell the food, listen for the sounds of people going about their daily work. My scholarly research may have given me the outlines for the full picture, but now it becomes three-dimensional, and I take my place inside it. It is usually at this point that I begin to recognize feelings or experiences that are touched by the events in the text. I write them down, along with the many images and sounds and smells that strike me during this part of the process. It was at this stage in preparing the sermon offered below that I began to see my student Heath standing in the doorway in her chambray dress.

In between these times sitting in the study, I have one other intentional activity connected with my preaching: I take walks. Every text on preaching I've ever read recommends taking some time away from the sermon to let the material simmer, to let the creative juices run un-channeled, to let the Holy Spirit move in and stir things up. I find that I follow that advice, but (congruent with the rest of my spiritual life) I do it in spurts, not in a disciplined, extended way. I walk most days for an average of about forty minutes. I spend some of that time in conversation with God, talking about this and that, trying to listen. If I am working on a sermon, I pray for my congregation and ask God to give them a gift from the text for that day. I also ask God to give me a gift, to open my imagination to recognize how the Word nourishes and heals me. I pray for faith, and I pray for inspiration.

This conversation, like all my conversations with God, happens interspersed with moments of appreciating the garden in front of this house or the energy of the dog barking at me from behind that fence, checking my watch to see how long I've been gone, calculating how great this is for my body, and trying to solve the problems of the seminary where I work. But I've come to have faith that the Holy Spirit has a stake in these apparent "distractions" in my prayer time, and so I've quit beating myself up for not being Julian of Norwich.

I do have another quiet time that I sometimes use creatively. I commute twenty-four miles to work on one of the most congested stretches of freeway in America. I count on it taking me about forty minutes, if nothing out of the ordinary has happened out there. I don't like commuting much. But for eighteen years I walked about two blocks to my office, so I suppose now I'm making up for all that easy living. For years, I tried to block out my commute with books on tape; I tried to engage my mind in learning something while I drove. I still do that now and then, but much more often these days I listen to music. Lots of Mozart. Dvořák. Wynton Marsalis and Stanley Turrentine playing soft jazz. I think about my work, and if I'm headed toward a sermon, I think about that. But the music opens surprising doors and windows in the same way that the walks do.

Liturgical music works in that way for me, too. When Alan and I picked music for the worship service, we were, of course, beginning with the texts of the music—and so we chose, for example, a setting of the Magnificat for the entrance hymn. But the text is far from everything. I often begin humming the hymns that will be sung on the Sunday I am preparing for, and the tune works on my heart too. Perhaps I subconsciously hear the words—certainly when I break out into song in the car, the words come (with holes, but who's listening?). But the tune carries meaning, too, and offers yet another point of access for the Spirit.

I do try to consult with people when I am preparing to preach. I don't have a colleague group or a regular committee to work with, because the schedule of my preaching is too irregular. But I have a number of people who contribute often. A friend and I often take a short walk at lunchtime, and I'll check out my musings with her. More than once, too, I have called her at home in the evening to try out a full sermon. She is particularly helpful to me because she is not an academic, and she is what the Myers-Briggs personality test calls a sensate. I am a high intuitive-type, teaching mostly other high intuitives, and I can enjoy too much my open-ended, follow-my-nose approach. My friend Margo helps me to be concrete. I also carry in my imagination a friend from an earlier life who heard judgment in absolutely every biblical text you could pick. I try out my ideas on her and try to hear her objections to my too-facile promises of grace or forgiveness. I have a friend in my Sunday congregation who is a prophet and something of a civic revolutionary, and sometimes I try ideas out on her—either literally or in my imagination. And I have a husband who is a Lutheran pastor and the chaplain at a prison for the mentally ill. He doesn't like to help me with my sermons, because we think so differently that we both get frustrated; but sometimes, early in the process, I can trick him into helping me by asking an innocent-sounding question about a theological or scriptural point that's baffling me. He catches on pretty quickly, but often not before he has given me a reaction that stirs my creative soul.

Sometime in the course of my musings, I usually become conscious of my hermeneutical spectacles. As I said, my husband ministers to some of society's refuse, and his ministry keeps me aware of those we marginalize in our churches as well as in the greater community. Someone pushed me not too long ago to identify a scriptural text that was the basis for my understanding of preaching, and immediately I replied, "Luke 4." By virtue of my baptism into Christ and my calling as a preacher, I understand myself to be following the model of Jesus (and Isaiah), called "to bring good news to the poor...to proclaim release to the captives and recovery of sight to the blind, to let the oppressed go free, to proclaim the year of the Lord's favor." I understand that mission both literally and meta-phorically. In terms of my preparation process, it causes me to ask myself, "What are the forces that imprison the people I will preach to? What oppresses them? Where is their poverty? their blindness? Am I offering a word of liberation to them from God?" And usually, to stay honest and to soften my heart, I also ask God to remind me of the forces—and the sin—that imprison me.

Up to this point, my work on the sermon has been in the direction of opening up, receiving, listening for guidance. Usually this part of the process takes most of the week, and I only begin to shape an actual sermon in the last day or two before I preach. I used to feel frustrated with myself that I always left the writing "until the last minute." More recently, I have begun to recognize how I actually work and to depend on the long period of meditation (for that's what it is) that is, in fact, the bulk of my preparation. Collecting the data, the images, the exegetical curiosities is easy and fun. But it is in the waiting—waiting on the Spirit—that those many components of my week of thinking and praying move from being separate entities to becoming a message, an event. I can collect all the elements in the bell jar, but the spark that catalyzes them comes from somewhere else, and—alas—on its own schedule.

The simple fact is that I do not have full control of what eventually emerges as a sermon. The final day or so, as I take my seat in front of that blank computer screen, can be full of anguish and self-doubt. At the very least, it is a time full of mystery. My students ask me all the time how to do this part, the actual pulling together of all those ideas and hunches and unformed intuitions into a message that has some direction and applicability to real people. I can explain what I mean by focus, and I can talk with them about form and style. But where the content comes from, how to find those analogies with familiar life that make the scriptural text hum in tune with our secret prayers and longings—I wish I knew. If I knew, my own composing would come more easily. If I knew, I wouldn't have to wrestle with angels almost every time I prepare to preach. If I knew, I wouldn't have to stop myself during almost every preparation and consciously hand my will over to God to be broken again.

In my study I have a lot of stuff on the shelves besides my books. At the moment I have taped to the shelves three clippings that I printed out from Web sites. One is a photo of Susan B. Anthony and Elizabeth Cady Stanton. You know the shot, I'm sure—there's Susan dressed in black up to her earlobes and down to her knuckles, looking scary; and there's Elizabeth in silk and ruffles and curly hair, looking like Grandma about to invite you in for a piece of pie. Next to them is a sort of standard but pleasant-faced portrait of Phillips Brooks. And next to him is Ernest Shackleton, wearing his Antarctic explorer's gear and looking at me with a steady gaze. Sitting on top of my printer is a plush toy version of Phil, Hercules' personal trainer from the Disney film, and next to him is an action-figurine of Princess Leia in her rebel-leader costume. As I look from computer screen to Bible to commentaries through the course of the week, I am also now and then glancing at these folks. I leave it to you to imagine why I chose them to be consultants on my preaching.

There are more members of that chorus in my study—pictures of family, little gifts from friends and students, an old crucifix. They remind me that they—and God—love me no matter how "well" I do in my preaching. They help me let go of my need to perform brilliantly, and focus me on being faithful. At some point in my process, I always have to return, one way or another, to the knowledge of that love, to my reliance on God's grace, and to my own calling as preacher, teacher, priest, and Christian. It is sort of like reciting the Hippocratic Oath before entering the operating room.

I try just to write. I try not to worry about form or style as I blurt out the ideas that have been steeping all week. After I've produced a page or so, then I look and see what's there. A direction may have emerged during one of my walks, and I may just note that somewhere. I may put it at the end and keep backing up from it with the other ideas that pour out (or that I squeeze out like blood through a pinprick). I may start with a question I've been mulling over and just keep writing to find out what the answer is. I keep praying through all of this. Often the "answer" turns out to be a reframing of the question; when that happens, I try to build a sermon around that moment of insight, so that the congregation may delight in the surprise just as I have.

Once I've figured out what the sermon is trying to be, I start carving away extraneous material that only serves to confuse. The cartoonist Sandra Boynton has been a great help to me here. In her book *Chocolate: The Consuming Passion,* she describes the "old-fashioned" way of making a chocolate rabbit. She says, "Stand on end: 1 block of chocolate, 4 x 4 x 7 feet. Chip away all pieces that do not contribute to an overall impression of rabbitittity."[5] The parts I chop away are still chocolate. They can be melted down and used again or just nibbled on for my personal enjoyment. But at this point the rabbit is what's important.

The next to last thing I do in preparing a sermon is edit it for style and format it (oh, the wonders of the computer!) into an oral manuscript. I use a full script for my preaching, which I depart from depending on my ease with it. I use a full script because I can't trust myself to stay on target without one. But I prepare a manuscript that is oral in style and easy on the eye (*big,* clear print). I talk my way through what I have composed, and I ask myself throughout if this is the way I would say it if I were teaching a class or chatting over a cup of coffee. I try to find a style that is colloquial and truly oral (short, sometimes incomplete sentences; lots of images; a certain amount of repetition; simple transitions), but still dignified. If I find that I am trying to say something that won't *go* into oral style, I prune ruthlessly or get rid of it.

I am a mediocre but happy pianist. A few years ago, after a long time away from it, I inherited my mother's grand piano, and I began to play again. Certainly, I was worse than rusty. But the amazing thing was that my fingers seemed to remember where to go for that old Chopin waltz from my youth, that bit of Scott Joplin I had learned to pound away at in my young adulthood. My body held the memory of how to make the music.

So the very last thing I do in preparing a sermon is practice it. Out loud. More than once. I practice it from the exact form of the manuscript that I will be using "for real." This isn't just about gaining comfort with reading the words, although that is certainly important. It is about hearing my own voice say the words that I have put down, letting my ears ring and my very bones vibrate with the sermon. I am teaching my body the music, so that when the time comes, I can sing it confidently, naturally, from the soles of my feet and the depths of my innards.

After the service has begun, there is little time for last-moment prayers. But I have been living with the texts and humming the hymns for a week, and so as they are read and sung, I enter into the larger prayer of which my sermon is a part. And because my conversation with God all week has been in the context of walking and deep breathing, as I plant my feet solidly behind the lectern and take that last quiet, deep breath before I begin speaking, I am letting my body recall the prayer that has informed everything I am about to say.

Homily for the Feast of the Visitation[6]
Luke 1:39–49

It didn't happen all that long ago. I was sitting in the faculty lounge at The Church Divinity School of the Pacific, eating a turkey sandwich. Across from me, eating an egg salad sandwich, was Jane Maynard, my friend and the director of our field education program. We had been relaxing, eating our lunches, and chatting about this and that.

Just then, there was a voice at the door. We turned toward the sound, and there, framed in the doorway, was a young woman, one of our second-year students. She was standing there in her blue chambray dress, a dress she wore a lot in these latter days, so as not to spend too much money on maternity clothes. And all over the skirt of that dress there were wet splotches. Her eyes were round and her voice was breathy with wonder and fear and joy, and she said, "I think my water just broke! It happened in the Dean's Office!"

My friend Jane left her lunch where it was and took the student into her office to call her husband, and then saw that she got to her apartment. I just stayed in the faculty lounge and finished my lunch. Now and then I glanced over at Jane's egg salad sandwich with two big bites taken out of it, and I prayed for Heath, for her husband Peter, and for the baby who was on the way.

It was okay with me that Jane went with Heath and I didn't. I'm not a mom. I've never been through what Heath was experiencing. But Jane *is* a mom. She has two kids, teenagers now. And at times like this, it makes sense to turn to someone who has, as we say, "been there and done that." Somebody older and wiser, maybe—a parent, a mentor, a guide. And if there isn't a family member at hand to take that role, we choose someone else to guide us, and that someone *becomes* family of a sort, through the relationship created by the sharing.

Do you suppose it was anything like that when Mary hurried through the hill country to the home of her kinswoman Elizabeth?

It's early evening. Elizabeth comes out of her house into the courtyard, carrying a cooking pot she's filled with a vegetable stew for dinner. She puts down the pot and lowers herself carefully down next to the fire, and she pokes the coals to make sure they're ready. Just then, at the edge of her vision, she sees some movement in the doorway. She looks up to the open door of the courtyard, and there she sees a young woman, framed by the doorway. The veil over her head is arranged neatly, but there are streaks of dust on it, and there's dust on her skirt, too—a lot of dust.

And the young woman's eyes are round, and her voice is breathy as she says, "Elizabeth! I'm going to have a baby!"

Elizabeth freezes for a second; she looks in amazement at Mary; then she begins to move. She takes hold of the corner of the house where she was sitting, and drags herself to her feet, and then she walks to where Mary is standing. Only then does Mary take in what *she* is seeing: Her cousin Elizabeth is pregnant, too, just as the angel has said—almost *seven months* pregnant.

The tears well up in Mary's eyes, and she steps toward Elizabeth. And Elizabeth takes a step toward Mary, and the child inside her gives her a good kick. The Spirit of God fills her with wonder and awe, and she cries out a blessing. And the two women embrace, and they talk excitedly about what has happened to them, and they sing, and they weep, and they praise God for mercy, and for miracles, and for freedom, and for the promise of great things to come.

I'd like to know a lot more about the relationship between Elizabeth and Mary. For instance, when Mary learned that she would bear the Son of the Most High, why did she go to Elizabeth, rather than to her own mother? Of course, Luke doesn't tell us any of that, because he's doing his own thing. The scholars say that Luke is using the two annunciation stories to build up to the miraculous births of John and Jesus. He's using the birth stories themselves to sort of sound the trumpets for the beginning of their ministries of prophecy and healing and liberation. It seems that really what Luke was interested in was having the two boys, John and Jesus, have a kind of encounter even before they were born.

Fair enough. But there they are, Mary and Elizabeth, both pregnant. And they're embracing in wonder and joy, and they're sharing stories about angels, and they're singing about God's faithfulness to Israel and about God's faithfulness to *them,* these two lowly women. And Luke lets them sing a long time, and he doesn't have anybody come around and rebuke them for making too much noise or calling attention to themselves.

The scholars also say that you're not supposed to make anything of the fact that the gospel says Mary stayed with Elizabeth about three more months. You're not supposed to do the calculations and figure out that Mary would have had to be present when John was born. It's not part of what's important to the narrative, say the scholars.

But I just can't let go of this picture: The younger woman standing in the doorway of the older woman's home, in wonder, and fear, and joy, looking for the support of someone older and wiser, a mentor, a guide. And the young woman finds instead an older woman who is also pregnant for the first time. And the older woman is filled with the same wonder, and fear, and joy, and so they become *sisters* in the awesome miracle of it. They become *sisters* as the Holy Spirit dwelling in one of them greets the Holy Spirit dwelling in the other. They rejoice together, and together they sing a song. That's the picture I can't let go of.

And of course you already know why this picture is such a powerful one for me. Because it describes so beautifully where a professor of preaching lives. It's such a wonderful, awesome thing to encounter someone who is pregnant with the Word of God. And a preaching professor gets to meet people like that almost every day. People like you.

The preaching professor knows that it's her job to be the guide, the older, wiser one, the mentor, the one who has been there and done that before. But the wonderful thing about this job I have is that those students who come to me pregnant with the Word of God help me to give birth, too. The songs I hear from them give me the music for the unsung songs of my own heart. The Holy Spirit dwelling in them calls forth the Holy Spirit dwelling in me.

Now, it's just possible that there are one or two people in this room who are secretly afraid that everybody *else* is pregnant with the Word of God except *them.* Their stomach is in a knot and their hands are a little sweaty, because they're secretly afraid that somebody made a mistake choosing them to come here this week, afraid that they only got to come because the Dean or somebody liked them. It's even possible that some of the *faculty* at this conference are afraid of something like that. But just to draw out this pregnancy metaphor as far as it can go—maybe *beyond* where it *should* go—let me say that that feeling in the pit of the stomach is part of the natural process. Morning sickness goes with pregnancy, even when you're talking about being pregnant with the Word of God.

All of us gathered here at this conference are pregnant with the Word. We're Mary—young and humble and awestruck by an encounter with an angel. And we're Elizabeth—getting along in years and suddenly renewed by a miracle from God. We come seeking someone *else's* experience to guide us, and we stay to play the midwife as *they* give birth. Nobody's really the old hand, it turns out. And nobody's really the rank beginner. Because—talk about old hands!—the One who dwells in us is the Word that has never been silent since before the world began; and talk about rank beginners!—the One who gives us voice is the Holy Spirit that is forever young, forever fresh, forever new.

Let's trust that. Let's trust that in each other.

CHAPTER 5

Yvette
Flunder

I am a desperate preacher who knows personally how theologies are fluid, and new ones are born at friction points. My voice is rooted in the African American Southern Pentecostal Church, where passion for God in Jesus is heard and seen in the songs, preaching, dancing, and daily at-home meditations. I have struggled with the history of the church and the interpretation of the Bible, but not with the freestyle celebratory worship of the Pentecostal Church. My struggle has been with the Christian church's position regarding the treatment of women, same gender–loving persons, war, people of color, and slaves (my grandmother Bessie Hamilton, born in 1895, was the daughter of Stella Wyatt, who was born a slave).

I am an avowed womanist and a reconciling liberation theologian who dances in the Spirit and speaks in tongues. Holding on to Jesus in spite of the church's tortured interpretations of scripture—used to mortally wound my people and my faith—has been a life-long journey. Finding my way, following the Light, refusing to believe that Jesus didn't love me/us—this is the foundation of my preaching. Mine is a voice that passionately preaches justice and freedom with responsibility; however, not to the exclusion of Jesus. Justice without Jesus will not work for me.

I preach to a desperate people, who are struggling to make sense of their lives on the margins of society. They are my beloveds. In my community, you must find God in the struggle for equality, parity, and justice. That struggle is the long, strong, deep, resonant bass line of all I preach, sing, and pray about. "Through many dangers, toils, and snares" is our theme—the foundation of our worship and the locus of our passion. If we cannot see God in the struggle and believe day after day that God will make it all right, then we cannot see God at all. This is the starting point.

I preach faith-based sermons to build self-worth and self-value in the lives of people who have often been stripped of all that is right and good. I strive to make peace and a sense of security present in the lives of those I serve. As Emil Thomas said, "Our slave ancestors had a basis for calm: a special inner peace born of a profound conviction that their self worth had been well established already and was guaranteed by the Ruler of the universe."[1] The peace that Thomas speaks of is a peace born from the assurance that God will come through for us—that God is on our side. This is what I believe; this is what I preach.

Homiletical Approach

I identify with homiletician Fred B. Craddock's approach to preaching. It is so Bible-, Jesus-, and God-centered. I've seen the methods he recommends for sermon structure used both in the United Church of Christ, where I presently serve, and in the Pentecostal churches of my youth. Although I am not in total agreement with the extent to which Craddock lifts up the authority of the Bible, I do appreciate and believe strongly in the kind of scripture-based, Christ-centered preaching for liberation that he advocates. With David Buttrick, I would argue for a church "animated by the Gospel, rather than a church heavily under the rule of an imposed scriptural authority."[2] People who have for generations been abused by the preaching of the Bible need to hear the Bible preached in ways that affirm and validate them. This kind of preaching requires study—and an eye to taking Jesus back from the fundamentalists—but it is the most effective kind of preaching for my community.

Preaching in my tradition uses life experience, or what I call "personal transparency," to identify with the experiences of the listener. It is important that the preacher be sensitive to the needs of the listener—that is, sermons should speak for, as well as to, the congregation. The gospel is from the community as well as to it. There is also a need for honesty and intimacy, and it is important to preach using themes, hymns, and stories that are familiar to the listener. I believe that in order to genuinely be a blessing to the congregation, the preacher must seek to know and understand who she/he is preaching to. In *Preaching as Local Theology and Folk Art,* Leonora Tubbs Tisdale calls this "exegeting the congregation":

> If we as preachers are going to proclaim the Gospel in ways capable of transforming congregational identity, we first need to become better acquainted with the ways our people already imagine God and the world. If we are going to aid in the extension of myopic vision or the correction of astigmatic values then we must first strive to "see" God and the world as our people do.[3]

It is through this synergistic relationship that the preacher and the congregation become one organism, worshiping God together. The preaching and the response are then filled with faith, passion, and power. This is preaching, as I understand it. New and difficult truths should be packaged in a familiar wrapping, so a common relationship of trust based on collective experience can be established. Preaching that is outside of the theological, intellectual, or cultural reach of the listener is an insult to the life experience the listener brings to the preaching moment. It is not enough for me to simply be profound; I must seek to be a profound blessing, by hearing from God and paying close attention to the "voice" of the listening congregation.

My preaching is greatly influenced by my grandfather, my father, my uncles, my mother, and my grandmother, all of whom are/were preachers. I spent my youth as a pastor's kid in the Church of God in Christ, a predominately black Pentecostal denomination. My style of preaching echoes the preachers who surrounded me, both in my family and throughout the organization. Most of the preachers I knew were blue-collar folk who came to their role as preacher and/or pastor without the benefit of formal training. There were not many African Americans in college, and if they were in school, they were seeking a way to make themselves more eligible for jobs. The call to preach was not often planned as a vocation. It sort of ran up behind you and tackled you while you were trying to get ahead in life. Authorization for ministry came from the church at such time as it was determined one was ready. "Ready" meant having demonstrated faithfulness and an ability to preach. The Church of God in Christ believed that no matter how educated or filled with deep knowledge a person was, that knowledge had to be evidenced by good preaching for a preacher to gain affirmation from the church.

Good preaching meant good performance that included choosing a good text, a good reading of the text, good entertainment, believability/authority, identification, food for thought, power, humor, passion, and a super celebration. I know that Craddock's statement "Listeners tend to lean into narratives which have emotional force, but which are presented with emotional restraint"[4] is an indication that we come from different cultures. Emotional restraint was not exercised in the preaching of the Pentecostal church—particularly at the close or celebration time in the sermon. I tend to agree with Frank A. Thomas regarding celebration and emotion. Thomas writes, "It is precisely because so much of Western preaching has ignored emotional context and process, and focused on cerebral process and words, that homileticians most recently have struggled for new methods to effectively communicate the Gospel."[5] In the church of my youth, preaching was central to the worship experience; it was the highlight. All things led up to it and out from it. It was a Word from the Lord.

I am fascinated when I read books like Richard Ward's *Speaking from the Heart,*[6] which describe the performance model of preaching. It is a model I recognize—one often present in black Pentecostal preaching. I find myself wishing that my Grandpa Eugene (Bishop Eugene E. Hamilton) and my Uncle Rudolph (Bishop S. Rudolph Martin) could have lived long enough for me to share with them the fact that a science is being taught that captures what they did among us for many years. Although they did not adhere to any particular preaching calendar or make much use of sermon helps written by others, the power of their sermons lives on.

Of particular interest to me is the "science" and skill of black Pentecostal word-smithing. I can see it now so clearly as I look back on the preaching I grew up around. I know that most of those folk did not realize what masters they were in the art of using illustrations, simile, or hyperbole, but all these things were part of their preaching process and, by inheritance, part of mine. Storytelling, speaking in hieroglyphics, and word pictures were methods employed to leave a lasting impression on the hearer. You could see it, taste it, and feel it while they preached. My Grandpa lived his sermons, so his ethos and personal conviction came through with great passion, energy, and emotion.

The Pentecostal preaching influence is one in which the language is ordered, the lines are metrical and poetic, and the sermon is "sung" in places with the help of the congregation and the musicians. This form of performance art entertained the congregation while driving home the truths in the sermon. Engaging the audience in a call and response to both the meter and the message not only encouraged the congregation to participate, it signaled that the sermon was successful. Preaching as performance art was and is an essential part of the African American Pentecostal worship experience.

Preparation

Reading is a passion for me. I read history, literature, scripture, magazines, Web articles, newspapers, and anything else I can get my hands on. In my reading I listen for themes of freedom with responsibility, hope, perseverance, culture, and real people. I look deeply into the characters in scripture for their humanity and how they identify with us. I want to demystify the saints without losing respect for their struggle. I seek to know by revelation and through literature contemporary with the text, what things the writers and interpreters did not tell us. We all keep secrets, so what would they rather we did not know? What is it they assumed we would understand? What meanings have been lost or changed with time? What is the truth under the writings? I seek to bring those things to the preaching moment.

I never know what I am going to preach from one Sunday to the next. The sermon subject matter comes through a song I hear, or a scripture or a book I read, or an experience I share with someone…some word or principle comes to my attention and my spirit says, "ah-hah, that will preach." I tend to write the thought down on anything that I can find, because I know it is preaching fodder. I experience great joy when a fresh Word comes to me for my people, because I know God is communicating with my spirit. I often don't do anything with the thought for a time; I just let it sit and simmer in my spirit, while I think and pray about the scriptural and human context for the sermon. There are often two or three sermon pots simmering simultaneously, and the last one may be first and the first one may be last. Other things come to witness to the truth that has already been deposited in me. The scriptures, examples, parables, and stories that bring the thought to life come in waves, when I am bathing, driving, or working on something else. I keep something handy to write with all the time. I have little notes everywhere that I accumulate when I come to my computer to pull the sermon together.

When the sermon is ready to be preached, it is always brief on paper, because I know I will get the rest of it in the pulpit. I need the people and the Holy Spirit working in the preaching moment to finish the sermon. I have often taken the same notes with me to different occasions and preached totally different sermons.

As to the content of my sermons, I often preach sermons to raise the consciousness of those who feel they have an exclusive right to Jesus and to empower oppressed people to take their place at God's "welcome table." I preach to build faith and to demystify success for oppressed people. I do not consider my preaching adversarial or divisive. I call myself a "reconciling, liberation theologian," because my desire is to see harmony in the body of Christ.

Empowerment and liberation are consistent themes in my preaching. Marginalized people often ask, "Is God for us?" Incarnational, liberating preaching is vital in these communities as an antidote to the kind of preaching that has often been used to push oppressed people more and more to the margin. In such communities, the preacher's approach or style evidences the extent to which the church is welcoming. After a natural disaster, people come to church in record numbers, asking, "Is God for us?" and then they listen for the assurance from the pulpit. In marginalized communities, crisis is a way of life, and incarnational preaching is essential.

Preaching to people who are on the edge of society and the mainline church must have good content and good form. Preaching to marginalized people must be believable, powerful, and passionate. Marginalized people frequently have a memory of strong words from the pulpit used to destroy. They need stronger words of affirmation and inclusion. In my sermons I attempt to carry a message that counters the teaching of those who support a theology that calls anyone unclean or claims to have exclusive "truth."

I believe there must be a relationship between loving and knowing God, the text, and the people the text is shared with. When the interpreter of the text begins by incorporating integrity, relatedness, and faithfulness to a relationship with God and to the text, there will be a more honest relationship with the congregation/listeners. Additionally, preachers must be secure in their relationship with God and witnesses of the truth of the gospel. Oppressed people seem to be particularly aware when there is disparity between what the preacher says and what she/he really believes.

Marginalized people are people who need to hear from God. How can they hear without a preacher? And the preacher must love God, love the text, and identify with the people in order to be authentic. When these things come together, I believe we achieve the moment of "transformation." I seek for this moment in my preaching. I have no greater joy than to embody a liberating truth and to participate in the circle dance as the Holy Spirit brings life to me and to those who receive the Word. When God in Christ through the Holy Spirit empowers the preacher and the congregation through the embodied Word, the circle is complete and the kingdom is revealed. It is a glimpse of heaven.

Managing the Thorn
2 CORINTHIANS 12:1–10

I. The Thorn: "A thorn was given me in the flesh, a messenger of Satan to torment me."

Paul had a problem. It was something that brought him great sorrow and perpetual embarrassment. It was connected to how he was perceived by people. It probably caused people to say, "Look at him. He talks faith and power, so why can't he free himself from this thing? Why doesn't Jesus deliver him? It must be something he is doing wrong." It made him look weak when he visited the churches. It made him the brunt of jokes, and some rejoiced at the suffering because they despised Paul's gift. It often caused him to defend himself by lifting up the work he had done and the miracles wrought through his ministry. (We are inclined to defend ourselves constantly when we feel misunderstood, as it says in 2 Cor. 11.)

Whatever it was, it was a constant irritation that kept his attention and threatened to distract him from the work of ministry. He had constant thoughts and prayers about how much better off he would be without the thorn, how much stronger he would seem, and how much more respected he would be. Apparently Paul believed that prayer would move this thing, perhaps because he had seen such deliverance come to others he had prayed for. Paul sought the Lord in private, probably embarrassed to tell others what he was seeking deliverance from. Why could he not get free?

The Source

This thing—this thorn—this aggravation—was prescribed by God and administered by Satan. All that Satan does to us must be with permission, which indicates the final outcome (Isa. 54:16–17). It was God's gift to Paul. God used Satan to stop Satan's own plan for Paul. What was Satan's plan? Same as it is for us. To use the thorn to distract, discourage, depress, and eventually stop Paul's effectiveness and ministry. Satan always believes he can defeat God's purpose. I think that is part of his curse, the delusion that we will be destroyed by the power of suffering. Satan doesn't seem to know how suffering empowers us. Never feel envious of anyone's abundant spiritual gift, since God, of necessity, attaches a messenger of Satan, an errand imp, with a designer thorn to keep pride in check.

The Purpose

The purpose of such thorns is to teach spiritual dependence. Liberty is one thing, independence is quite another. To be liberated is to be free from the restrictions wrongfully placed on us by another. To be independent is to be free from every tie and dependent on nothing or no person. It is also a delusion and a fallacy. We are all dependent on something or someone in some way…possibly the doctor or the plumber who knows things we don't know and we must depend on their skill. And if nothing else, we are dependent on God, for in God we live, move, and have our being. All of us ought to be free, but none of us ought to even seek to be independent.

The spirit of independence is a spirit of pride. The potential for Paul's pride was located in his gifts and revelations. Even before he came to know Christ, he was a formidable man, skilled in the law and languages…probably an overachiever to compensate for his perceived weakness. But on the road to Damascus, while seeking to demonstrate the extent of his commitment to the law, his culture, and his God, Paul met Jesus in a great spiritual experience. After he came to know Christ, he continued to experience powerful revelations and was given great gifts for the purpose of his calling. He was to go to the Gentiles and expand the boundaries of the faith to include those who were thought of as unclean. A new and living way was coming alive in Paul's spirit, and he had great insight and vision. He was the man who was called to write most of the New Testament, and his life journey would affect believers for generations to come. With all of this Paul had to be tempered and balanced, or he would have had the potential to spin out of control…to float away full of pride like a hot air balloon without sandbags. Spiritual pride is the worst kind. And if Paul, as pious and deep as he was, needed a thorn, how about us?

God intended the thorn, not as a stumbling block or a hindrance, but as a catalyst for Paul's power and authority. God cannot truly use us until we are consciously weak before God, until there is no shadow of doubt who is in control, until we get out of competition with God for God's glory. It was important that Paul understand what rejection felt like if he was to effectively minister to the rejected, and he could not do the work of ministry in Asia Minor while constantly boasting of his experience in the third heaven. God set this pious Pharisee up by allowing him to first be ill-received by the brethren because he persecuted the saints; then God subjected him to the thorn. The thorn led Paul to earnest prayer—the kind of pouring out of the soul that goes beyond pretense. What would turn us to this kind of prayer but a thorn? And Paul kept calling until God responded.

We have great gifts. We are designers, poets, singers, musicians, health professionals, lawyers, clinicians, computer whizzes, and so forth—so much collective wisdom and ability and so many thorns. What is keeping us from turning the world upside down for Christ? The fear of the thorn. The thorn says, "Don't get too far out there or I will come out and embarrass you and put you to shame. Keep your dreams and expectations minimal and small, and maybe the real issues won't be noticed. Don't be too transparent, or you'll be exposed."

Where we have missed our victory is in allowing the thing to constantly defeat our forward mobility. We feel that because we hate it and because it is a messenger of Satan, then God must hate us when we are not free from it. So why won't God set us free? God can but won't. The thorn has moved from being a tool for our growth to becoming an object of perpetual distraction. It is "overcoming time."

II. The Promise: "My Grace is sufficient for thee."

Grace is God's favor, not given to us by our merit…we could not earn it. Grace is the heart of God extended to us and the power of God made available to us. Grace makes us able to be what God commands us to be. Grace both insures our victory at the end of the journey and walks with us day by day. Grace cancels out sin's power and penalty in our lives.

Grace, *charis,* is the opposite of *hamartia,* or sin. We cannot be both under sin and under grace (Rom. 5:1–2). Grace cancels out the power of sin and brings us into close fellowship with God through Christ, where we have access to all spiritual gifts in Christ. Grace enables us to press toward God's standard for our lives and then makes up the difference when we miss the mark. Grace will make it all come together and work together for good. Grace takes the chance out of our eternity with Christ. God's unmerited favor and pardon will carry us through, no matter what our weaknesses are. We are justified by faith and kept by grace. The gifts that come with justification and salvation have no relation to human merit; they are eternal and are wrought by God. What are some of these grace gifts that God gives us because of Christ's sacrifice?

We are the elect of God and precious.
We are the chosen.
We are the called.
We are redeemed.
We are reconciled.
We are forgiven.
We are free from the law.
We are the children of God.
We are regenerated.
We are born again.
We are adopted.
We are made acceptable to God.
We are made righteous.
We are positionally sanctified (holy).
We are perfected forever.
We are justified.
We are delivered from the power of darkness.
We are translated to the kingdom of Christ.
We are a gift from God to Christ.
We are inducted into the royal priesthood, chosen generation, and holy nation.
We are citizens of heaven.
We share in Christ's inheritance.
We have the Holy Spirit as our guide and seal.
We are complete in Christ.

What need have we to have the burden removed if God will give us the sufficient grace to bear it? What does the weight of the burden matter if the strength is equal to bear it? Why be pulled from the fire designed to make us better servants before we are refined if God will give us the requisite grace to endure?

God's grace is sufficient for what?

Our labor, which often discourages us;
our struggles, which often frighten us;
our suffering, which often depresses us.

We can depend on the grace of God to be sufficient to make us glory in our tribulation, because we are assured of God's presence and power. Why shrink back from our call because of our weakness when God's power is made perfect in it?

This eliminates using the thorn as an excuse to neglect our call and destiny. Sufficient grace is not a promise to those who sit and moan about the thorn but to those who go on in spite of it. Depending on God's grace brings us into unity with our selves…it integrates us and helps us to give the process time. Grace expands the narrowness of religion by setting us free from fear of divine retribution and giving us room and time to grow into the full will of God for our lives. Knowing that we have God's favor changes our hearts and minds and lives. Grace gives the poor wondrous patience and trust.

Grace makes the sick man or woman more concerned about ministering to the visitor than complaining about the sickness.

Grace woos the angry violent man and calms the beast within.
Grace loves the hell out of us.
Grace holds us like a womb—safe while we grow.

We can go though the valley of the shadow of death by the grace of God. It is sufficient for whatever we must face. Extraordinary grace comes with extraordinary challenges and will not manifest itself until you are in the struggle. It is easy to believe in past grace and hope for future grace, but trusting that God is holding us up in the middle of the mess is a true challenge to our faith. But know this…

Grace is unlimited.
Grace is unmerited; you cannot earn it, and it is a gift with
    Christ's purchase of us at Calvary.
Grace is making your trouble useful to you and making you
    triumphant over it.
Grace is prepared to bring you out of a thousand more
    difficulties just like this one, until you see Jesus.

Grace is sufficient to avert whatever would harm you.
Grace is ready to supply whatever is good for you.

This wonderful power can only be revealed and clearly seen when we are in trouble. How else would we know that we can be kept through anything until we go through something? God's strength is made perfect or at its highest potential when we are weakest. You see grace at work when Jesus said, "Forgive them, for they know not what they do." Look at the people Jesus chose to work through: a Gentile doctor, some fishermen, a tax collector, a harlot. Someone said that Jesus' ministry would not last six months, but Jesus and his folks and the many who followed turned the world upside down. Look at us. God can use people who know that they need a savior. We do our greatest singing, our greatest preaching, our greatest writing, and our greatest giving when we are weakest.

You may read about the grace of God in the Bible or in books. You may hear about it in a sermon. But you don't know about it until you are in desperate need and God comes through. When our weakness is thoroughly felt, then the strength of God can be made perfect in us. The strength of God is not perfected until our weakness is perfected. That's where some of us are now, in the process of having our weakness perfected. Our stuff that has been buried and squashed is coming up and out. It is oozing out of hidden places, and folk are seeing who we really are. Now that we see it won't help to get mad or depressed, or to cover, or to blame, maybe it is time to surrender the weakness into the hands of the only one who loves us in spite of everything and see what Jesus intends to do with the rest of our lives.

III. The Resolve: "Therefore I will all the more gladly glory in my weaknesses..."

Paul had tried desperately to succeed at being a righteous man and felt that he had failed miserably. He still could not make the war in his flesh nor his thorn go away (Rom. 7). He suffered until he received the revelation of faith, grace, and power—reoccurring themes in his writing. Faith as the path to salvation, not works and rituals; grace, or God's unmerited favor, unending love, concern, and enablement; and power from Christ to both will and do after God's good pleasure. Paul saw the end of the journey, so he was able to put the present squarely in the hands of Jesus.

Paul had earnestly desired the thorn to be removed, and now just as earnestly he desires to let it remain, rejoice in it, and leave it to God's grace. Paul received a completely new view of life. He learned a new lifestyle: how to manage his thorn and not be managed by it was the source of attaining the power of Christ. Paul wanted the power of Christ to rest or dwell on him, not touch him and go.

Paul came to understand what true power is. We are tempted to admire power based on human definitions of power. Great conquerors and rulers get human attention. King Saul of old got the people's attention: He was strong, he was tall, he was handsome, and he was a great warrior. David got God's attention. He was a shepherd, he was small, he was young, and he was weak by human standards. What was the difference? Saul trusted in himself and witches; David trusted in the Lord. The Lord was his shepherd, and the Lord made him greater than all his adversaries. Even when he failed God, God still called him a man after God's own heart. Who but God can turn a curse into a blessing—making the very thing that used to bring such sorrow now a source of greatest joy?

Christ was called gluttonous, a winebibber, and a devil, yet he kept his eye on his purpose, not on the slander. He did not adjust or change anything in his plan based on what the slanderers said about him. Christ is now the one friend that slander cannot alienate…nothing said about us will drive Jesus from us (Rom. 8:38–39).

Paul gloried in the thorn. We can glory in the thorn, because it makes us tender toward those who also suffer. We can encourage them to look to God so that their suffering will have value. Because we all must suffer, our suffering should be for something. What greater value is there than to have the power of Christ rest upon us?

We can glory in our weakness, because while we are weak in one way, we are receiving supernatural strength in another. Just as the blind person excels in hearing and touch, the area where God wants us to excel is greatly enhanced by our weakness in another area. When God gets ahold of our weakness, it becomes another thing and works under another law. Our weakness is transfigured into strength. God not only helps us with our weaknesses, God transforms them into power.

Paul wanted the power of Christ to dwell, rest, or tabernacle with him in the same way that the Shekinah power dwelt in the tent in the wilderness. The Shekinah, or the visible residence and manifest presence of God's power and glory, was a cloud that rested over the mercy seat (or ark lid) between the cherubim atop the ark of the covenant. What was the Ark? It was a simple box of wood overlaid with gold. What was its significance? It was what rested on it. Paul was offering his weak and frail self as a habitation or a resting-place for Christ's abiding presence and power. He was making his storage empty and available to Christ. He was saying to Christ, "Rest on me, take up your abode in me, I don't want my need for glory and attention to stand in the way of your glory. Let me pass out of sight behind you. Take center stage, Jesus. Glorify yourself through me! I am just the lamp; you are the light. Shine Jesus shine! I am the dancer; you are the dance. Dance Jesus dance! I am the instrument; you are the melody. Sing Jesus sing! And I am just the temple; you are the Presence. Show yourself strong in me, Jesus, for your own glory! Amen.

CHAPTER 6

Mary G.
Graves

I am a preacher who has been shaped by growing up in the
Presbyterian Church; being discipled in my youth by Young Life and
Inter Varsity Christian Fellowship; experiencing a call into ministry
through Christian camping; being trained by Ian Pitt-Watson at Fuller
Theological Seminary in Pasadena, California; completing a doctorate
in spirituality at San Francisco Theological Seminary; and, most
significantly, being involved in preaching for the past sixteen years,
first as an associate pastor and now as a senior pastor.

The church I am currently serving is a flock of six hundred in the
middle of a white, suburban, high technology culture. The members
are mostly "married with children" and stable in their life circum-
stances, with a mixture of churched and unchurched backgrounds.
The staff I serve includes other preachers who can share the load,
with me preaching approximately 80 percent of the time. The style
of our worship is what I would describe as "blended," with a mixture
of the traditional and the contemporary. It is a highly educated,

"kid-friendly" congregation that values humor, anecdotes, and informality even more than I do.

As a preacher, I am committed to beginning with scripture and not a topic. Though the liturgical year automatically leads us into seasons of special emphasis, it is important to me that the biblical text provide the sermon focus. The choosing of each Sunday's passage is determined by many factors. The process of deciding on sermon texts happens at least six months in advance in order to accommodate the music staff, who have to buy their music and train their choirs (sometimes at fall retreats or summer music camps) well in advance of the Sunday on which they sing. In order to do this, the choir directors want to know the preaching texts and special events in worship (baptism, communion, Youth Sunday, Pledge Sunday, etc.) in June for the next church calendar year. It is difficult to plan that far out with certainty, but I give it my best shot and then allow myself the freedom to change it later, if necessary. The elements that contribute to my selection of the texts include the liturgical calendar (Advent, Epiphany, Lent, Easter, and Pentecost), our church calendar (stewardship, ordaining and installing church officers, missions emphasis, etc.), and the rhythm of the lives of the congregation (government holidays, Hallmark holidays, school holidays, and their vacation schedules).

Another very important part of my deliberation is how and when to use the lectionary texts for that year. Our Sunday school curriculum, *The Whole People of God,* follows the lectionary, so I consult the lectionary texts first in thinking through my preaching year. I value the purpose of the lectionary, which is to prevent us from returning to favorite and familiar sections of scripture while avoiding the whole of scripture. However, many times the lectionary starts a book study at an inopportune time, such as in August when our folks are vacationing. Or it doesn't provide for a timely opportunity to speak to the events of our times, like the turn of the millennium. Therefore, I let the lectionary serve me; I don't feel obligated to serve the lectionary.

I enjoy doing *lectio continua,* preaching through a book of the Bible. I think this helps our biblically illiterate culture feel more familiar with scripture to sustain interest from Sunday to Sunday and to lend itself to an accompanying adult education series. In addition, it saves me the extra work of doing background work on a new book each week. When I do this, I try to make sure I represent the diverse literature in the Old and New Testaments, alternating back and forth between the two. I will recycle material I have used in the past at strategic times when I know I need to be more freed up for other demands on me as a pastor. For instance, I was understaffed last year and was scheduled to teach an in-depth Lenten Bible Study series on Wednesday nights. During that period of time I preached a series on Ephesians that I had taught in my previous church. It was a big help.

Sitting with the Text

Once I have selected a text, I spend time in it alone. I do not try to include all the lectionary texts in my thinking. I would rather be deeply immersed in one passage than broadly attentive to several. I also try not to let the passage be too long, for my sake and for the congregation's. I begin by writing the text out by hand on a pad of paper. This practice helps me engage in the text, word by word. Once it is written out I look for repetitions in words or phrases or other marks of special emphasis and contrast. Much like *lectio divina,* I let myself notice on my own what the text lifts up. I try not to rush this step or skip it altogether, which would be very easy to do. Pastors never have enough time. Before I read any other opinion, I want to see what the text does with me.

Studying the Text

I have a host of commentaries I have collected over the years, some more valuable than others (I especially like the *Interpretation* series). What is valuable for me is scholarly study combined with practical themes. Even commentaries that I don't agree with theologically can still be helpful; I don't dismiss them automatically because they are too conservative or too liberal in their approach or their conclusions. I try to purchase commentaries that are inclusive in the breadth of their research and ones that begin with the premise that scripture is the inspired word of God.

I bring home the commentaries I need, because I do my study and sermon writing at home, where I am less likely to be interrupted (I live alone). My study begins briefly on Monday morning to provide me with just enough information to put together the order of worship and decide on a sermon title, which then goes in our marquee on the corner. The bulk of my study is done on Wednesday morning. I wish I could do all my study and sermon prep before the order of worship is put together, but there are two things that prevent that. First of all, the order of worship needs to be crafted by me on Monday for the sake of the office staff and in time for our all-staff meeting on Tuesday. Second, I have found that I cannot focus on more than one sermon at a time, so I cannot seriously pursue the content of the next sermon until the one I'm working on is already preached. So by the end of Monday morning I am pleased if I have been able to write out the passage by hand and skim a few commentaries.

I do not work with the original texts, which I know is a great disappointment to my seminary professors. Occasionally I will do word studies, but I am dependent on resources that explain everything in English. The same is true with the commentaries I use. I don't mind the scholarly works as long as they don't expect me to understand the Greek sentence they just referred to without providing me with the translation.

I usually check between four and six commentaries, thoroughly reading and underlining the ones that have helpful insights to share and skimming the ones that are repeating the same points. Then I write notes on what I've gotten from the commentaries. This process on Monday and Wednesday normally takes less than three hours, unless I'm starting a brand new book in the Bible and need more general background.

Ruminating on the Text

The next step in my process is about breathing time. My regular day off is Thursday, the day after I have completed my study. I do not attend to the passage or the sermon at all on my day off, at least not consciously. I definitely take a day off. But I have come to appreciate the unconscious simmering that goes on as I carry the word that has been planted in me the day before. Something is growing invisibly in the inactivity of that Sabbath space.

The Emergence of a Theme

On Friday I read through the passage and all my notes, underlining and then listing the main points. I become very intentional about asking, "What is the main point being made here?" Sometimes the theme is right there, already formed in my mind. Other times it needs more ruminating time, so I go for a walk or take a shower. These are creative thinking times for me, and they help "midwife" what is being born.

As the core thought emerges, I write it down as my "focus." I like it to be one sentence in length, something easy to understand and grab hold of. Often this focus statement goes through many drafts before I feel that it captures what has risen to the surface through my studies. The most difficult part is keeping it simple, not trying to include everything that came up in my research.

Applying the Text

Once the passage has been reduced and simplified to one core thought, I work to expand the "so what?" At this point I search for illustrations and what I call "emotional equivalents" that communicate the theme to the congregation. I try to work on the development of the theme, which takes the form of an outline. This outline is also greatly influenced by the illustrations I have chosen. I have found that the sermon pivots on what the people can image and feel rather than on what they hear.

When I say "emotional equivalent," I mean a parallel in the listeners' lives that helps them *feel* what the biblical writer wanted his or her readers to feel. I want my listeners to "get it" at a gut level and not just at a cerebral level. This requires that I step into the writer's world and wisdom first and then step into ours—at an emotional and experiential level. I have noticed that this is something important in my preaching preparation that is not necessarily primary for others.

The illustrations I use are taken from many sources: what I observe around me in real life, what I have collected and typed up on index cards and filed away topically in card boxes, and illustrations taken from book compilations (e.g., by *Leadership Journal*). The collecting of illustrations is critical, because that is often the only thing my listeners will carry away with them. It takes an observant mind and intentional effort to find them and save them in a way that makes them accessible when you need them. It is also important to keep track of when you used an illustration so that you don't keep repeating it. I pencil the date on each illustration card I use and put it away in a separate file once used. I wait a few years before recycling one I've already used.

Writing the Sermon

It is my normal practice to script out my sermon, hopefully in a way that matches the way I talk. I type it into a pre-formatted template on my computer that produces 5 x 7 inch single-spaced pages, which fit easily inside my Bible and are easy to move around in the pulpit without people noticing.

My goal is to get a rough draft written by the end of Friday morning so that I can rework it on Saturday morning, but that rarely happens. More often than not I spend my Friday morning coming up with the focus statement, developing an outline, and then searching for illustrations. Then I am in the unhappy position of writing and rewriting and rehearsing the sermon all on Saturday, which is exhausting.

I am a morning person and do my best work before noon. So I plan Friday morning and Saturday morning to finalize the flow and to write. I also work best when I'm not trying to produce a finished product the first time around. My first draft needs to be a rough one, or else I will get bogged down with each paragraph or thought and never get the thing done. Once I have a rough draft, I can look at it as a whole, evaluate the flow, and make big and little changes. I have also found that working only on a monitor screen does not work for me. At some point I need to print out a hard copy of the rough and rework it from there. The editing is then done on the computer, which always takes more time then I think it will.

I have learned how many half pages of sermon text it takes to make a twenty-minute sermon: six, single-spaced. I aim to preach twenty minutes, fifteen if it's communion Sunday. That represents a reduction from my earlier years in preaching, when my sermon would last twenty-five to thirty minutes. Pressures on worship and recent data on what people can absorb have led me to the twenty-minute guide.

Rehearsing the Sermon

My sermon is not finalized until Saturday evening, usually before dinnertime. It is my preference to review it at least once in its final form before I go to bed (9 p.m., if I'm lucky!). I say "final form," but I keep revising the sermon until it's preached, though I don't make substantive changes at this point. Substantive changes mean having to get back on the computer, which I avoid doing late on Saturday.

I have found that making social plans on Saturday night is a mistake, and I generally avoid doing so. I need to pour all my attention into worship and preaching the next morning. I review the order of worship and remember the context for the preached word. Then I read what I have, try to live with it, and go to bed. No sermon ever feels completely finished; it can always be improved. At some point I have to tell myself, "I can preach this," and trust God.

I get up quite early on Sunday morning (4:45 a.m.) in order to pray, get ready, and have at least one hour to speak the sermon out loud twice before arriving at the church by 8 a.m. Lately I have been reading it to myself before I shower, thinking about it in the shower, and then saying it out loud twice if I have time. I don't say it aloud in front of a mirror, but I do practice standing up and relating to my notes on my kitchen counter as if I were in the pulpit. I don't try to preach without notes, but I do try to preach so that I'm freed up from my notes and establishing eye contact regularly with the people.

When I first began preaching, I liked to rehearse in the sanctuary pulpit. But I found that I was often interrupted. I could not count on that space being available, so I started doing my practicing at home. The difficulty with that is when I have company on a weekend, it's very hard to find enough privacy to say the sermon out loud without my guests hearing. I can't give up that Sunday morning rehearsing time, though; it's critical for the last lodging of the sermon inside me.

Preaching the Sermon

By the time I enter worship and step into the pulpit, I'm preaching what I have prepared and am able to do it with confidence. I rarely add or delete pieces. Sometimes I will elaborate a bit more during the second service (our church has two worship hours back-to-back) when I don't have to be as rushed, but basically I stick to my well-prepared and prayed-over script.

I haven't lost my sermon notes yet, though they disappeared briefly between services one Sunday when a worship leader inadvertently picked them up with her own notes and threw them away. There was a desperate scramble that made my heart skip a beat before someone found them and returned them before the next service.

Preaching practicum students asked me recently if I get nervous when I preach. When I was an associate pastor preaching six to eight times a year I did get nervous. But since I have come to this position, where I preach most Sundays, I don't feel nervous. There are times when I feel unprepared and out of focus, but I don't experience the inner butterflies I used to have before standing up to preach. I have had to mentally coach myself to enter into the experience with confidence and joy because this flock needs to hear this word. It's my way of loving them. It helps me to focus on their need and not on my self-consciousness.

Revising the Sermon for Publication

We make our sermons available in print (eventually online, too) the week after they are preached. This requires me to go back over the sermon after it is preached and revise accordingly on my computer, because many of my changes are written by hand on my sermon notes. The revised script is reformatted for full-page publication and put out on the literature table at church the next Sunday.

Miscellaneous Notes

Many people in the congregation ask me how long it takes to prepare a sermon. My typical response is between fifteen and twenty hours from beginning the study to getting up to preach. I do not use study groups or feedback groups as a part of my sermon birthing process, though I can see how valuable they would be. It is mostly an issue of time and access to the right people to make it work. My longing is for a study group that would focus on the liturgical seasons of Advent or Lent and help me to prepare in advance with lay leaders in liturgical art. I would gladly make time for something like that.

The Sermon That Follows

After taking time last summer to check the lectionary texts leading into and through Lent, I planned to do a series out of the gospel of Mark. This was the gospel selected by the lectionary, but I changed the chronology of passages to fit our preaching schedule. During the second week of the series I began my preparation for preaching on Mark 1:29–39. I was a little shorter on time than usual Monday morning as I skimmed through the passage and a few of the commentaries in order to prepare the order of worship by midday. A cursory overview of the passage showed that Jesus' fame was due to his acts of power, healing, and casting out demons. Yet he was not enamored of fame as most would be; in fact, he feared that it might get in the way of what he came to do, which was to work a greater healing than what initially got people's attention.

I let myself think about the topic of fame. We had just emerged from the pomp and hype of the Super Bowl. One of the football stars who surfaced in that game was the St. Louis Rams' Kurt Warner, an enigma to the press because he was such an outspoken disciple of Jesus Christ who couldn't care less about fame. He had experienced a sudden and completely unexpected rise to superstardom in that game but wasn't much impressed by that. I started saving articles about Kurt Warner and the game, something I knew everyone had been hearing about in the news, even if they didn't like football.

At the same time, the country was in the thick of a presidential primary in which each candidate was trying to outdo the others, competing for the limelight. So the topic of fame was in keeping with current events. It fit, too, with the initial clarity that came from the text. I felt safe in designing worship and crafting the sermon title with that theme in mind: the allure of fame and how it had nothing to do with what Jesus came to do. I titled the sermon "Jesus Christ Superstar," which went up on our corner marquee on Tuesday. I was sure I had my hands on some great illustrative material with Kurt Warner and the presidential primaries.

Deeper Study and a New Direction

My brief interaction with Mark 1:29–39 on Monday gave way to my expanded time of study and reflection on Wednesday morning. As usual I entered into the text first by writing it out by hand and letting myself notice each word and phrase. Then I went back and made notations of everything I noticed. This step also included looking at the passages that preceded and followed my pericope. Jesus' stated purpose in Mark 1:14–15 ("The kingdom of God has come near… repent…believe…") was key in contextualizing in verses 29–39. I started noticing Simon Peter's part in this story, both as a participant all the way through the narrative and as a contributor to the Marcan message.

I then glanced through all my commentaries, focusing only on Mark 1:29–39, because I already had done some background study in the gospel of Mark. I wrote down what seemed noteworthy in the commentaries. What surfaced consistently was the "from Peter" perspective, and I began to entertain that vantage point in my imagination. In fact, I got so excited about presenting a sermon from Peter's point of view that I interrupted my note taking and started writing a flow based on Peter's first-person perspective. It stemmed from the narrative of Mark 1:29–39 but also encompassed all of Mark and what Jesus came to do.

I knew we would be celebrating communion that Sunday, and I imagined Peter's narration culminating at the table. I was still working with the same focus I had entertained on Monday morning: Jesus' quick rise to fame because of all of his works of power and healing, and the danger of missing the deeper healing that Jesus came to bring.

It was a radical thing for me to be considering a first-person sermon. I had only done that once before, and I knew that it placed different demands on the preacher. It was also difficult to let go of the great illustrations I had already begun to collect early in the week, because those are always so hard to come by. Also, this new direction made the sermon title, "Jesus Christ Superstar," a little less perfect than I'd originally designed it to be, and it was too late to change it. But I knew I couldn't pressure myself to write a sermon to fit a title I'd created with only minimal contact with the passage. I decided to let it all go, and I went for a walk. During that walk even more ideas came to me for the first-person sermon. I wrote them down and then let them lie fallow through my day off the next day.

The Struggle with Preaching a First-Person Sermon

As far as I'm concerned, in order to preach a first-person sermon, you have to get out of the pulpit with no notes and engage the people. You have to draw your listeners into the speaker's perspective by making the narration believable and your presentation compelling. For me that meant not only putting the sermon together well, but learning it so well that I could get up without notes and not be self-conscious. I wasn't 100 percent sure I could do it.

Then there was the increasing "peer pressure" I had been feeling to go note-less and pulpit-less. Many of my pastoral colleagues are seeking to improve their preaching in this way. They are filled with a sense of accomplishment when they can step away from the pulpit and speak directly to the congregation with no notes, or very few. That is their ultimate goal in preaching: to preach note-less and pulpit-less. In my own estimation their definition of progress has less to do with content than with delivery, and I find myself resisting what feels like a "selling out to an entertainment culture." I believe in a strong delivery, where you are freed up from your notes and engaging in constant eye contact, but I would rather invest the bulk of my sermon prep time on the content.

I knew it would take more time for me to prepare a first-person sermon, not to compose it, but to learn it. Because it was communion Sunday, the sermon would need to be shorter, so that helped. I would have less to learn. Also, the main transitions of the emerging sermon flow were big and clear, and I knew I could remember those even if I didn't recall everything else.

I was compelled to preach this sermon from the perspective of Peter's experience of Jesus. It would do justice to the narrative and the point of the passage. I decided to risk it. It was good for me to try new things and good for my congregation to experience new ways of hearing.

The Final Preparation

I kept my focus statement before me at all times: We are attracted to Jesus' spectacular healing power and can miss the deeper healing he came to do. With that core thought printed in the upper left corner, I wrote out my outline of what Peter would tell my congregation.

My next step was to fully script the sermon, first a rough and then a final draft. Then the learning process began. I had to find a way to make this message my own. I read through it several times on Saturday afternoon and started reducing it to an outline again. I broke it down into major blocks that I could remember, stepping stones that would remain in my mind and guide me from the beginning to the end. I refused to go to bed on Saturday night until I had some inkling that I could remember a basic flow of what Peter was going to say.

Sunday morning, I went through the sermon out loud several times and let go of my need to remember everything. I no longer referred to the script, only to the main blocks in the flow. This sermon was going to depend on my being Peter and sharing his experience, not my trying to deliver a memorized speech of Peter's. So I reassured myself that I knew enough of what happened to Peter that I could say something meaningful, even if I lost track of everything else I'd planned to say. Worst case scenario: I could get us to the communion table, and Jesus would redeem it all.

I was nervous when I started the sermon, but it went great. I entered into Peter's skin and found it moving to talk at a personal, experiential level like that. My congregation was quite spellbound. I couldn't tell if it was because they were shocked that I was doing something unusual, or because they were engaged in Peter's testimony. The feedback I received at the door was a mixture of both. The sermon made a big impact. They were moved by Peter's account and impressed that I presented his message the way I did. More people commented than usual, and for many days afterward.

I still resist the prevailing philosophy that says note-less and pulpit-less is the only way to go. But I am glad I ventured out of my comfort zone and tried something that was so challenging—mostly because it was true to the text and to the way God was leading me to preach it.

Jesus Christ Superstar
MARK 1:29–39

I would like to introduce myself to you. My name is Simon—Simon Peter. I was one of the Twelve who lived and traveled with Jesus during the last three years of his life, which was an amazing time. In fact, the gospel of Mark that you just heard is pretty much based on my remembrance of that time.

That is why I'm here. I want to explain to you in more detail how confused we all were about Jesus at that time. I think it's easy to be confused about who Jesus is and why he came. But I don't want you to be confused, and I don't think Jesus does either. So I want to tell you what happened to me.

When we first met Jesus, it didn't take long to realize that he had power to do amazing things—I mean amazing things! But we had no idea; we were not able to grasp the even more amazing thing he actually came to do. We could see right away that he could heal anybody of anything, but we had no idea what kind of bigger healing he came to do.

The passage you just read in Mark was really the first day that we saw Jesus' power, and it just about blew us all away. We had just been in the synagogue in Capernaum, and Jesus was teaching in a way that was so different from what we were used to. His teaching hit home. You could see it on people's faces. You could feel it in the room. Everybody could feel it, and they were all looking around, thinking, "Who is this guy?!" They were so impressed.

But they were even more impressed with what happened next. Before Jesus was done speaking, this man in the crowd stood up. He had a wild look on his face, and this strange voice came out of him. Everybody could tell it was the voice of an evil spirit. And this voice spoke directly to Jesus. We didn't really know what was going on, but we all thought Jesus was in trouble. You don't mess with evil spirits.

But you know, Jesus wasn't intimidated at all. In fact, he looked directly at that man and commanded the evil spirit to come out of him. All of a sudden the man started screaming and shaking like he was having a seizure. We were all scared to death! Then before we knew it the whole synagogue was calm. The evil spirit was gone.

Everybody was in awe. Nobody could stop talking about what Jesus had just done, the fact that he actually had power over evil spirits. None of us had ever seen that kind of power before. It took us a long time to get out of that synagogue; it took us a long time to get Jesus out of there, because everybody wanted to be near Jesus. But we finally left and came to my house in Bethsaida.

The first thing I was told when I walked in the door was that my wife's mother, Anna, who had been living with us for a while, was really sick. I could tell just by the look on my wife's face that it was bad. Anna had a high fever and couldn't even get out of bed. Jesus was standing right there, and when we told him about Anna's fever, he didn't hesitate. He walked right over to her bed and took her by the hand.

I'm telling you, she was as limp as a wet rag. She could barely acknowledge Jesus' presence. But as soon as he touched her, something happened. I can't tell you how it happened, but the fever and the sickness just left her. Her color returned, her energy returned, and she practically sprang out of bed raring to go. It was unbelievable. She started waiting on us, especially Jesus, as if she hadn't been sick at all!

It was amazing to see Jesus' power at work. Of course, it didn't take long for people to hear about it. Word spread like wildfire. And by the time the Sabbath was over, which was at sunset that day, all these people were gathering outside my door with every kind of problem you can possibly imagine.

I looked out there, and I saw people who were crippled. There were people who had been burned half to death in a fire. I remember seeing a little child who had been stung by a scorpion. There was everything: injuries, sicknesses, people who couldn't see, people who were possessed. Some of these people I recognized, but a lot of them I'd never seen before. There were hundreds!

And Jesus was amazing! He wasn't overwhelmed by this at all. He spoke to them one by one and touched them one by one at the door of my house. And every person he touched walked away healed. Over and over again, into the night, we watched the same thing that happened to my mother-in-law happen to them. We watched the same thing that happened to the man with the evil spirit in the synagogue happen to them. Eventually, we had to send the people away, because they needed to get some rest and so did we.

It was an unbelievable day! It was the first day that I saw Jesus' power at work. No wonder he said he came to bring good news! No wonder he said that the kingdom of God had come near in him. It was obvious that God's hand was upon him! I figured that Jesus had to be so pleased with how his ministry was getting off the ground. He had barely begun, and he was already so popular!

But boy, was I surprised with what happened the next morning. I wasn't surprised to see the crowds back. I knew they would come back. I wasn't surprised when people started knocking on the door before the sun even came up. But I was surprised when I went to get Jesus and he was gone! Nobody knew where he was. We looked everywhere.

Finally, after the longest time, we found him sitting all by himself in a secluded spot outside of town. I couldn't figure out why he was there. I asked him, "What are you doing here?! You've got a whole crowd of people looking for you!" You know what he told me? He told me he wanted to leave. He wanted to leave all those people waiting outside my door and go to the other villages, so that he could tell them the same message he had told us.

I couldn't believe what I was hearing! His ministry was just beginning. He was an overnight success. Why would he leave?! I thought he had come to draw a crowd like that. I thought he had come to be their leader.

In that conversation I could tell that Jesus didn't really like the fact that he was becoming famous. He didn't want to make a name for himself; he didn't want to be a superstar. He wanted to move on. There was something greater that he needed to do.

None of us could understand this. We had watched him change people's lives; we had seen him do amazing things! But we couldn't begin to grasp the amazing thing he actually came to do, which wasn't about being famous and popular. It wasn't about bringing temporary relief to the suffering people outside my door. He could do that. He could heal anybody of anything, and at first we thought that that was what his ministry was all about. We just had no idea what kind of deeper healing he came to do and what it would ask of him to do it. None of us could understand that until it was all over.

When I saw Jesus heal Anna in my home, I became a true believer. I had known that there was something great about him the first time I met him; that's why I followed him. But when he touched her and that fever left her, I knew I would follow him anywhere. That healing changed my life.

It's interesting to look back on that now, because at that point I just could not see the greater healing that Jesus wanted to do. I could not see the deeper healing that Jesus came to do in Anna's life, which was not about the fever—it was about setting her free to enjoy him and to serve him. I could not see that he came to heal a deeper sickness in all of us that keeps us from living for God. And I couldn't understand it until he did it for me.

It's hard for me to admit this, but of all the twelve disciples I was most impressed with me. I knew I was one of Jesus' favorites. I knew I was the strongest leader in the bunch. I knew I was more passionate and more dedicated than the rest, or I thought I was. I was very impressed with my commitment and my loyalty, and I figured I was about as close to Jesus as you could get.

Then Jesus called my bluff. One day he was trying to tell us, warn us, that he was going to be arrested and killed, and I shot back immediately, "Over my dead body!" No way would I let anyone ever lay a finger on him, even if I had to die to protect him. Well, Jesus shot back at me. He rebuked me for trying to keep him from going the way of the cross. Little did I know that that was what he was praying about when I found him all by himself early in the morning back in Bethsaida. He was praying that God would help him do what God had sent him to do, to go the way of the cross, not the way the crowds wanted him to go.

After Jesus rebuked me, the next thing he said to me stunned me even more. "Truly I tell you, Peter, you will deny me three times before you hear the rooster crow." When he said that I thought, "How could you have so little faith in me?" I was devastated.

But I was even more devastated when I soon found out that he was right. I was not able to be faithful. I was not as loyal as I had promised to be. In his darkest hour I couldn't stay awake with him. I didn't protect him. In fact, I denied even knowing Jesus, three times. When I heard that rooster crow, it was the lowest point of my life. I had failed him. And I didn't just deny him, I denied who I really was, because I loved Jesus more than anything or anyone. I completely failed him, and I failed myself.

But after all the horror of his death and after the shocking news of his resurrection and then proof that it was true—I experienced the deeper healing that Jesus came to bring. It was the first time he stood before me, face to face. He didn't say a word about my failure. Instead, he asked me three times if I loved him. Each time he asked "Peter do you love me?"—with tears flowing down my face I told him I did.

And then he welcomed me back into ministry, just like that. My worst betrayal ever, the worst moment of my life, when I turned my back on God, was forgiven and healed. That's when I understood the deeper healing that Jesus came to bring. I wasn't confused anymore. That's when I understood the good news that he came to proclaim to everybody and to accomplish on the cross. That's when I understood that he came to heal all our unfaithfulness to God. I understood, because he did it for me.

As you hear about the incredible healings that I saw Jesus do and that he still does, it's easy to want that and only that from Jesus. We want him to touch the pain of those we love, the pain we experience in our own bodies and in the world. Sometimes he does and sometimes he doesn't, and it's easy to be confused. I don't want you to be confused about who Jesus is and why he came, and Jesus doesn't want you to be either. But I have discovered that the only way we can understand who Jesus is and why he came is by what we are given at this table.

I know it sounds crazy; it sounded crazy to me when he first told us during that Passover meal that "this is my body broken for you" and "this is my blood poured out for you." We didn't know what in the world he was talking about! And we didn't want to know. But after his resurrection, then we knew. I knew. Then we all knew that it is only in Jesus' body broken and his blood poured out that we are given the most long-lasting and spectacular healing of all—healing with God and with ourselves and with God's world.

For so long I was convinced that Jesus' greatest act of healing was Anna. I know it sounds silly, but it meant so much to me and my wife and our whole household! But I've got to tell you, Anna got sick again that next year, and she died the following winter. There is a deeper, more long-lasting healing that Jesus came to give to this world. It's the healing he gave to me. And I believe he gave it to her. And I know he came to give it to us all. He came to heal us from everything that keeps us from loving the Lord our God with all of our heart and soul and mind and strength, and our neighbor as ourselves. That's what Jesus came to do. Praise be to you, Lord Jesus! Praise be to you, O Savior of us all, for the life and the healing you have given to us, which never ends!

CHAPTER 7

Linda Carolyn
Loving

I have a love/hate relationship with preaching. Always have, always will. I hate preaching the most when I go to bed at 9:35 p.m. on a Saturday night, knowing that other "real people" are out seeing newly released movies or flirting over a plate of Pad Thai or having a glass of wine at intermission, and I...I, the preacher for the next morning, am crawling into bed pretending that I am content with my sermon and pretending that I will sleep. (Instead, I surf through dreams in which I can't get to the pulpit because I'm trapped in the church basement just as I hear the strains of the Introit; or I step up to the communion table and discover that, instead of bread and wine, it's chips and salsa...or brownies and milk, depending on what I had for dinner.) I love preaching the most when I am singing the closing hymn at the second service and know that in forty-five minutes I will be in my sweats at the Louisiana Cafe reading the *New York Times* and eating hash browns and letting go, letting go...knowing there is nothing more to the sermon except that, by the grace of God, someone who heard it is somehow living more like Jesus. Definitely, a love/hate relationship. Not a pretty picture; perhaps not a wise way to "position" myself, but there it is.

The "birthing" metaphor is an especially meaningful one for preaching. How often do women get the *real* story on childbirth? If someone who has heard me preach asks me immediately afterwards if I would consider a guest preaching gig or publishing a sermon, I routinely say, "Not good timing. It's a little like talking to a new mother in the labor room about sex." I don't mean to be unduly irreverent (or perhaps I do), but it's taken me years to make peace with the fact that writing sermons is a bear and that it takes a lot out of me. At the same time, I simply cannot imagine my life without this rhythm of creative angst and then relief (and don't forget the hash browns!). I simply cannot imagine my life without the privilege of this burden. A major difference between sermon writing and childbirth is the lack of labor coaches surrounding you into the late nights—no one "on call" in the next room, no one watching for signs of distress, no one holding your hand and telling you how to do it. Just me and my laptop and the cats (Joe and Isaiah) and Bach on the CD and pots of French Roast. For an extrovert like me, this writing is isolating indeed, an ultimate spiritual discipline that keeps me totally dependent on the Holy Spirit as the only coach I truly need (once I have done my exegetical homework, of course!).

As alone as I am in the crafting of a sermon, there are the voices—a whole chorus, speaking in many tongues. I call them my pentecost of procrastination. The first few years I was preaching I would sit down (at a typewriter in those days) and count out ten blank pages (I triple-space for easier delivery) and put the first one in the typewriter and stare at the blankness of it all and suffer from a state of "snow blindness." As I stared and stared, I would start to hear the voices. Natalie Goldberg, in her book *Writing Down the Bones,* refers to them as "the editor";[1] Anne Lamott, in her book *Bird by Bird,* claims that "perfectionism is the voice of the oppressor, the enemy of the people...[it] will ruin your writing, blocking inventiveness and playfulness and life force."[2] (Both Goldberg and Lamott have been midwives for me, along with Kathleen Norris and Barbara Brown Taylor.)

The voice of my mother, soft-spoken as she is, has been the loudest. I remember Sunday noon meals as a child when the sermon was dissected intellectually, cutting as close to the bone as my father's carving knife working the roast. (And those were outstanding sermons, by the way.) Then the voices of Miss Rotter and Miss McGlaughlin, who relentlessly drilled grammar into me in junior high. Then the voice of my older sister, who called me in my first year in ministry, in tears, saying, "Don't you ever, ever preach an irrelevant sermon that doesn't intersect with the lives of the people in the pews," after coming home from just such an irrelevant sermon at a time when she was in deep pain herself. Then the voices of all the left-brain male pastors I have heard preach brilliant sermons over the decades, making me feel insecure about my right-brain utilization of a children's story, or of metaphors and triplet repetitions. Then the voice of a retired theology professor who worshiped at my first church and would leave me hanging with obtuse comments such as "*That* was an *unusual* use of the text." Then, worst of all, my own voice saying uplifting things, such as "Who do you think you are that you can preach the word of God?" and "This is too simplistic" and "You always preach the same thing over and over and over again." Jack Stotts, retired president of Austin Presbyterian Theological Seminary and McCormick Theological Seminary and one of my true preaching "heroes," helped me over the last one by confessing to me on his way to the pulpit one Sunday morning, "You know, any one of us basically has one sermon in us." That became helpful counterpoint to the chorus in my head. There were other angels of mercy until finally one day, by God's grace, I realized the voices had subsided.

Okay. So now the voices had ended, and the silence was deafening. This was hard; this was good. No more preaching to please others, no more preaching in order to confirm my unworthiness. In the silence I learned to listen for the Spirit and for my God-given voice and to stay true to both. I also learned how to listen more intentionally for the Spirit's leading by seeking out ongoing spiritual direction and setting up a prayer corner in the same room in which I write. I learned to trust that I would, for no apparent reason, wander to my book shelf and pull down a book I hadn't touched in years and find just what I needed for the next paragraph. (And I am *not* a person who believes that God finds me parking places!) I believe that listening to the appropriate voices is a critical component of sermon writing. Medieval mystic Julian of Norwich has been my mentor, reaching mystically across the centuries as I bring her to life in a one-woman drama, *Julian,* written by J. Janda. Julian has taught me about the contemplative life and about theology; she also knew about voices:

> And as for me in all this silence I suffered from noise, voices in my head…Accusing voices endlessly telling me that I was responsible for all the evil and suffering in England. At times I could not hear my self or anyone else…the voices, the accusing condemning voices—they grew louder and louder till I cried out to God that he in his mercy would give me peace—to live, to stop the voices. God heard my cries, the voices gave way to silence…I could now stop my self-hating, my blaming, and turn my life to simple tasks which make for peace—my own—and others—and see, for the first time, the good in all—and see God in all.[3]

I believe that as preachers we are called to interpret and elicit the good in all, to see God in all. Not a Pollyanna preaching that excludes prophecy and pain, but preaching that is grounded in knowing, as Julian said, that ultimately "all shall be well; and all will be well and thou shalt see thyself that all manner of thing shall be well."[4] That is why we can preach to a church packed with mourners remembering the life of a seventeen-year-old lost in an unthinkable car accident two blocks from home on an ordinary Saturday morning. That is why we can wait patiently for a groom to say "till death do us part" when all gathered know he lost his first wife in a plane crash and is now unable to say the expected words. That is why we can preach about wars and famines and injustice that people don't want to take in…because we see the good in all, the God in all, and we know that all will be well. There you have it—my "one sermon."

If we have only one sermon in us, how creative and diligent preachers need to be so that the message is fresh week by week. I have gotten bolder about using children's stories and folk tales and art masterpieces as ways to connect us to the sermon text. This expansive approach came about by accident. One weekend I was moving into a new house and simply ran out of time, and in desperation I grabbed *Old Turtle,* because it was Earth Day—that and the Genesis creation story and I was home free.[5] Subsequently I have woven other children's literature into adult sermons, including *Emily of New Moon* at Easter, *The Glorious Impossible* at Christmas, *Love You Forever* for Ecclesiastes 3, *God Goes on Vacation* for Sabbath.[6] Madeline L'Engle's book *Trailing Clouds of Glory* is very helpful in making the theological link between children's literature and preaching.[7] In a way, whenever I write, there is a childhood mantra within—"I think I can I think I can I think I can"—from the book *The Little Engine That Could*. I loved rediscovering in midlife that the engine had actually been a *girl!*

I'm always on the lookout for sliding into a predictable formula, lest my sermons become a genre like romance novels or mystery series. Sometimes I spread the last several sermon manuscripts on the floor in a circle around me (like I used to do with my paper dolls) and make sure (as with my paper dolls) that I have a lot of variety. This way I can usually spot a trend—quoting too many women mystics and no scientists; too much humor, too little humor; top-heavy in personal anecdotes; not vulnerable enough; whining; blaming; and so forth. Although it's true that I let a sermon go once it's delivered, these occasional "overview" sessions are helpful indeed. Sometimes I find that I need to get back into the Old Testament, or need to write a "practical" sermon, or need to push us with a "disagreeable" text. The key is staying true to my own voice while varying the approach.

One way I try to ensure variety in my preaching is by taking in the world as the smorgasbord that it is. On the Enneagram I am a seven—"the Epicure"—a nice way of saying that I'm a glutton. I find tools such as the Enneagram and Myers-Briggs Personality Type Indicator and the Seven Chakras helpful to self-understanding—a vital quality for healthy ministry. These tools also enhance understanding of colleagues and parishioners; rather than pigeonhole people, they help expand ways to connect through preaching and pastoral care. So as a "seven," here is a sample of my smorgasbord: I read the *New York Times* and the local *Pioneer Press,* the local local local *Grand Avenue Gazette* (the personals give you a real flavor for what's on people's minds). I listen to public radio and go to first-run movies and read poetry out loud to the cats and try to read at least four bestsellers a month (two fiction, two non). I hit the museums on a regular basis—especially special exhibits. It's amazing how many sermon ideas are born in such a setting. I travel everywhere and anywhere at a moment's notice. Travel is how I have best come to know and love God's complex creation and creatures. The act of taking my passport out of the drawer is practically a sacrament for me, and the whole trip a kind of prayer. Travel feeds not only my spirit but my sermons as well (taking great care, of course, not to turn the gospel into a travelogue of what I did on my summer vacation. Back to the paper doll concept, I am vigilant to see that I am not dressing too many sermons too often with statements like "Last time I was in Bali"…).

Detached observation of people in all kinds of situations is another resource in creative writing and human understanding. I actually learned this discipline when I was studying theater in college, and an acting professor told us to spend a morning at Detroit Metro airport simply watching people say hello and goodbye. It was during the Vietnam War, and there were always people either saying goodbye or being reunited with loved ones in the service…gut-wrenching. There was, as well, the tenderness of other greetings and farewells, all carrying stories I knew nothing about. I observed so much humanity in the airport encounters of lovers, business partners, sorority sisters, and grandmothers seeing newborns. This kind of observation, a little voyeuristic perhaps, is a very quick study of the tenderness of the human condition. I still find myself in tears in airports practicing this discipline, and I think it helps me keep relevant to the heart of things when I'm in the pulpit.

Another resource that I'm never without is a small journal to jot down quotes, billboard ads, snatches of conversations I've overheard, lines from plays, metaphors that bubble up, moments in an ordinary day that seem to shimmer briefly with transcendence (often for no apparent reason except to find their way into a sermon later and really speak to someone else unexpectedly). I walk through my day as if I were a human magnet and see what I collect, but I need to be very disciplined about making notes or I lose track. What's especially helpful to my magnet is if I already have in mind certain texts coming up. On a really good day I even have files for those texts and then can rip the little notebook pages out and pop them into the appropriate files at day's end.

In shaping a sermon I almost always need a core image, a seed, a metaphor, a phrase on which to "hang" the sermon. I assume that most people start with a big picture or a map of where they want to go or an outline before they begin to write. I need something small to start with if I am true to my voice. Coming up with sermon titles for the newsletter a whole month in advance is incredibly helpful, because it forces that definition for me early on. Part of being a glutton means that it is helpful for me to narrow the universe of choices and *focus*. We are all so tempted to preach the *whole* thing. Again, I rely on the wisdom of Julian: "Life is a precious thing to me, and a little thing…and the world is a little thing, like a hazelnut in God's hand."[8] So week by week I look for the hazelnut and try to place it in people's hands on a Sunday morning. Some of my sermon titles reflect that practice: "Sleeping with Bread," "Of Quarks and Quirks," "Jeopardy, the Final Question," "Search for a Storm Home," "The Rainbow Connection." The clearer my focus, the stronger my magnet for attracting stories, quotes, materials that subsequently help develop the sermon. Rarely does the "hazelnut" confine; subsequent research and percolating can lead to a variety of directions.

Percolating. There's a concept. It has taken me a long time to affirm percolating time. I used to feel guilty when I was staring at a wall or rearranging my closets or listening to Taize chants on an evening in which I had "meant" to write my sermon. There is a difference between procrastination and percolating, and I admit that at times it's a very fine line. I am very grateful to finally have given myself permission to know that once I have the text and the "hazelnut," I am cooking without necessarily being at the stove (read computer). I wander through commentaries and periodicals (especially *Homiletics* and *Pulpit Resource*…); I phone, fax, and e-mail my brother and sister, who are also preachers. I percolate. Acknowledging the gift and need for percolating time has also helped me to trust that when I sit down to actually write, something will come. By God's grace. Always by God's grace.

The point at which I finally sit down to write is, unfortunately, still unpredictable. I have been all over the map on this and hope against hope that I am shifting into a pattern that results in a rough draft by Thursday night. For one thing, this allows percolating time on the *other* side of the process. For another thing, this allows me a sense of enormous freedom to be fully present to other things and people, because I know that *something* is down on paper and I can always "noodle" that. Otherwise, the unwritten sermon feels like such a burden looming on the horizon, a constant energy leak. A certain fear of the holy task ahead is important, but better if faced earlier in the week. This makes me less resentful or torn if something unexpected comes up on the weekend—whether a pastoral emergency or a set of baseball tickets on the third baseline.

At the same time, having a draft—even a "noodled" draft—never sets me free completely. The closer Sunday gets, the closer the cloud closes in…the free-floating anxiety that I can never quite shake and have tried to befriend. Part of it is that the sermon, because of the nature of preaching, feels unfinished until it is delivered. The challenge is to live with that "unfinished" feeling and not obsess about the sermon. All the relentless "noodling" in the world cannot eliminate that feeling. The sermon is simply unfinished until it has life and breath on Sunday morning, when the congregation is bringing their gift of responsible, faithful listening. In order to live with this "unfinished" feeling, I have learned that I need to get up very early on Sundays (usually 4:30 or 5 a.m.). I need to pray. I need to write in my journal. I need to do deep breathing exercises. I need to read through the sermon one more time with my red pencil…not so much to critique as to polish transitions, fine-tune word choices and repetitions, befriend what I have not liked in it. I do not allow major rewrites at that point. The early morning hours are intended for personal spiritual preparation, not production. And finally, I cry. Yes I do. I spent years thinking that I was some kind of wacko who was surely in the wrong business. Then one day it dawned on me (by the dawn's early light) that this is simply part of my creative process, and this is how I finally surrender the sermon to the grace of God. Then I blow my nose, eat my cereal, and go preach.

On my way to the pulpit, I have things I do that help me get centered. I sit in a pew for a few moments and imagine the sanctuary filling up with people who are hungry, whether they know it or not, for God's Word. Then I stop by the choir rehearsal for a few minutes and let the notes "hold me." I blow the musicians kisses. Then I walk through the Sunday school wing for my baby/child fix. Then I walk up into the pulpit to make sure everything is in its place. (We learned in theater classes that although there are prop masters, a wise actor always checks his or her own props.) I do not leave my sermon in the pulpit; I clutch it in my sweaty hands through two services and two coffee hours, and I have a back-up copy in my office. Next stop is to schmooze with the weekend receptionist to hear what's on her heart and make sure there's no crisis brewing to throw me at the last possible moment. There's a big difference between getting unsettling news twenty minutes before the service instead of two minutes. I have tried to train my clergy colleagues in this as well, so that they won't lean over to me as we start the processional to say something like "Did you see us on the morning news?" From the receptionist I go to my office, put on my robe and lipstick, do one more set of deep breathing exercises, load my pockets with breath mints, and then gather the staff in the chapel for a time of prayer before the processional. By now I know who I am and whose I am and where I am and what I am supposed to do, by the grace of God.

When I finally step into the pulpit, it is a relief to be there. I never underestimate the importance of feeling at home in the actual preaching space. Knowing where the light is, where the water is, where the microphone switch is. When worship leaders somehow communicate that they don't know what they're doing, it increases the anxiety of the worshipers and decreases their ability to be in the extra-dependent state that allows for transformation and the work of the Spirit. We are exhausted after we preach, not just because it is a workout but because as well we take upon ourselves in those twenty minutes the spirits of those listening. If we don't, we are merely performing or lecturing. We take on those precious spirits in order to be a mystical connection for them to the word of God. When all the exegesis and writing and rehearsing are done, that connection is what it's all about.

How we make that connection varies, of course, according to what our God-given voice is. Some people preach word for word from a manuscript; some preach from an outline; some use note cards; some use nothing at all, either speaking extemporaneously or memorizing completely their manuscripts. Making the mystical preaching connection with people is not as dependent on the mode of delivery as it is on ensuring that our mouths are speaking from our "guts." I mean this literally as well as figuratively. Too often public speaking comes from the throat and not from the diaphragm, and that weakens the impact of the message and makes the voice tight and tired. This constricted vocalization can especially be a concern for women, because one of the ways we meet resistance is through people complaining that "her voice is too high." Don't even give them the chance to "go there." (And while we're on this topic, wear shoes that avoid the complaint about "clicking high heels," and save your big earrings until you've won their trust, and take it in stride when instead of remarking on your brilliant sermon they ask you if you've changed your hairstyle.)

Another important dimension of delivery is eye contact. Genuine eye contact. Not looking above their heads at the exit signs. Not just looking at the smiling faces of your spouse or mother or best friend. Not scanning quickly. Not looking mechanically at the same four spots in the same order. Genuine eye contact. The key times of the sermon for genuine eye contact are during the opening paragraph, the closing paragraph, and any stories that might lie in between. I try to always have the most eye contact at those points and to know them by heart, and I have realized that many people think, as a result, that I don't use a manuscript, but I do, I absolutely do. I lovingly choose each word in my sermon and do not want to leave to chance intended images, rhythms, order, or phrasing, and so I absolutely use a manuscript. Each and every time. This may be a growing edge for me, lest I be too dependent on the manuscript or too prideful, or lest I use the manuscript as a shield against personal vulnerability.

Vulnerability in preaching is a huge issue. Head and gut must be connected, or we will not connect with our people. "It is out of the abundance of the heart that the mouth speaks" (Lk. 6:45). On the other hand, if we get *too* emotionally involved, we are not reserving the part of us needed to "take on" parishioners' spirits so that they can be in that extra-dependent phase. They start worrying that we're going to lose it or over-share, and suddenly it's not about the word of God anymore. Of course, preachers are not infallible, and it's dangerous indeed if we start communicating that we are, but when preaching, we need to keep it together for the most part. The toughest time I ever had was when I did a wedding for a woman who was getting married for the first time at the age of sixty-two. She was a friend, was an elder in the church, had been on the Pastoral Nominating Committee that called me, and was much beloved by all of us. The whole congregation had been invited. My homily was "in the can." On Wednesday before the wedding, she and her fiancé learned—out of the blue—that she had pancreatic cancer and only weeks to live. They decided to go forward with the wedding as if nothing had changed. They wanted no one to know in order for the day to hold as much joy as possible for everyone else. Friday night after the rehearsal I stood in the dark sanctuary and imagined Melissa walking down the aisle to the sound of trumpets. I imagined looking at a beaming congregation, knowing what only I would know. I stood on the chancel steps and wept. I tried to rehearse the homily and sobbed. I tried and tried until I got through it three consecutive times without crying, and then I went home for a good night's sleep, knowing I would do what I had to do by the grace of God.

Practicing sermon delivery is a highly individual thing. Because of my theater background I try not to "over-rehearse" so that I don't "peak at dress rehearsal." When I am teaching preaching, I always admonish students to practice in the pulpit ahead of time, and indeed most preachers I know do this. I do not. Because of the way I'm wired, I need to save that "edge" for delivery. Some people think that because I am an actress, sermon delivery is a breeze. Certainly my training is very beneficial for voice and diction and presence, but the truth is that acting and preaching are very different experiences for me. On stage I play another person, and I cannot see beyond the footlights. I am not responsible for the spiritual well-being of the patrons and usually never see them again. At the end there is applause and the knowledge that I have a chance to improve in tomorrow night's delivery.

By comparison, a sermon is a one-night stand. And it's the same costume over and over (okay, I get to change the stole color now and then). And instead of playing someone else, it's very important that I "play myself," which leaves me more vulnerable. And no footlights means I can see people yawn, leave, check their watches, whisper, make grocery lists. There is no applause, and in fact, I am very careful not to take Sunday-morning-feedback-at-the-door too seriously. People unfortunately often feel that they need to say *something,* and there's no opportunity for real dialogue. The feedback I find to be helpful occurs when the sermon has stayed with people long enough that they take the time to wrestle with it and write or call (with either positive or negative remarks). One of the most challenging things about preaching is that we often never know when we have had the greatest impact, and it is usually not dependent on one sermon but rather on a relationship and trust built between preacher and congregation. What a gift, what a blessing it is when people are hungry for God's Word and are eager to receive it through our God-given gifts.

My love/hate relationship with preaching is precious to me. I pray that the Spirit will continue to grace me each week with a "hazelnut" to impart as I continue to nurture and reframe the "one sermon" I carry within, intended for my voice alone. Every moment of every day shapes me as a preacher and I pray that I may be grateful all my days and radiate that gratitude and joy whenever I am privileged to preach. And now for the hash browns...

The Context for This Sermon

The Presbyterian Church (U.S.A.) meets annually in different locations for their General Assembly, where elected commissioners, lay and clergy, from around the country gather to "do the work" of the denomination in committees, plenary sessions, and voting. Each day begins with a worship service for all commissioners, staff, visitors, previous moderators, delegates, and so forth. In order to seat the more than two thousand people in attendance, the worship is held in a large hall or theater or arena. The "congregation" is diverse indeed, and in 1997 when this sermon was preached, the denomination was in a great deal of conflict because of the action of the previous General Assembly to approve "Amendment B," commonly known as the "fidelity and chastity" amendment, which requires all single people to abstain from sex and is, in particular, a lightning-rod gay and lesbian issue. Interesting to me was the feedback I received for several months after the sermon. Both "sides" of the Amendment B issue seemed to be able to connect in a positive way with the imagery of the church as nest, and several committee members conveyed that the metaphor was used in their work throughout the week of the assembly. This has helped me to trust all the more the use of metaphors in sermon preparation.

Bird's Nest or Hornet's Nest?

DEUTERONOMY 32:10–12

"It's time to leave the nest." "She's facing the empty-nest syndrome next fall." "Don't bother the newlyweds; they're nesting."

Curious, isn't it—all the ways in which a bird's nest serves as a metaphor for home, for family life, for nurture? We don't talk of the homestead as a lion's den or a bear's cave or a beaver's dam, even though we are closer to mammals than birds in the evolutionary scheme. No, we talk about nests.

Biblical imagery of birds is a common way of communicating our relationship with God. Our Exodus lesson soared with descriptions of God carrying the Hebrew people as if on eagles' wings. Our gospel lesson reflects Jesus' longing to gather us under his wings, as a hen does her chicks. Elsewhere in scripture we are comforted that not a single sparrow falls without God's knowing it, without God's caring. The Psalms proclaim again and again the refuge that we will find under God's wings. The metaphor of God as a mother eagle is most fully developed in Deuteronomy, where God's relationship to Israel is described as being like "an eagle [that] stirs up its nest, and hovers over its young…spreads its wings, takes them up, and bears them aloft on its pinions" (32:11).

Early life in a bird's nest is not easy. I have just come from Ghost Ranch, our denomination's conference center in New Mexico. This is my fifth June visit in a row—I try to plan it then so that I can watch the baby birds scrapping for life in the nests that seem to be everywhere: trees, eaves, Adirondack chairs—every nook and cranny. The baby birds, feathers not yet developed, scrawny necks reaching skyward, seek the mother's return with nourishment. When she appears there is a cacophony of high-pitched squeaks from gaping, fragile beaks, but the mother bird always remembers which bird she fed last and moves in meticulous order to the next one. I think many of us arrive at Ghost Ranch or other retreat centers or even General Assembly worship feeling very much like those baby birds, yearning

113

for nurture, starved for it, knowing that we can't truly survive without it. Baby birds exposed to the elements—whether a cold rain or a quiet cat—are almost pitiful in their vulnerability. Unable to fly, they are utterly dependent on the mother's return for food, warmth, protection, and eventual teaching when they are strong enough to fly.

In the one-woman drama on Julian of Norwich, by J. Janda, Julian—the medieval mystic, spiritual guide, and author—wisely compares the church to a nest, a robin's nest, "meant to protect the fledgling soul until it is ready to fly."[9] Julian claims that the mother bird is God's Holy Spirit. The church as a nest.

Nourishment, warmth, shelter, teaching, community. The bird's nest may well capture the second great end of the church, which is the "shelter, nurture, and spiritual fellowship of the children of God."[10] In all that we do as disciples, as congregations, as a denomination—we must never lose sight of that quivering vulnerability and primal hunger that we share, utterly dependent on the care and guidance of the mother bird. Especially at this moment in the Presbyterian Church (USA). We're all somewhat out on a limb by now, having taken impassioned stances on issues from Amendment B to COCU (the Consultation on Church Union, now to become Churches Uniting in Christ). We've been through a storm, which leaves us wondering (once the feathers settle) who's left in the nest, who has tried to fly, who has been pushed to the ground, who has been left unfed, whose wings have been clipped never to fly again.

Yet God's covenant began with us centuries ago, a covenant that promised that God will bear us up on eagles' wings; a covenant that promised that God will keep teaching us to fly until we can soar to God's glory, soar to heights we don't even dream of. God's covenant promises that there is room for everyone in the nest, in the shelter of God's wings. We participate in the covenant by cultivating our churches to be not gothic fortresses, not social singles' clubs, not "drive-through communion," but fragile, open nests, where all who are needy and vulnerable and hungry for spiritual nurture and truth can gather for safety and feeding and friendship. Room for all, *all*, in the shelter of God's wings.

Last fall I spent a long time looking at Rembrandt's painting *The Return of the Prodigal Son* hanging in the Hermitage in St. Petersburg. Theologian Henri Nouwen wrote an entire book on this painting. A great red cloak covers the bent-over body of the father as he welcomes home his wayward son. Nouwen compares the cloak to the sheltering wings of the mother bird and quotes Jesus' words: "Jerusalem, Jerusalem…How often have I desired to gather your children together as a hen gathers her brood under her wings."

Nouwen writes:

> Every time I look at the tent-like and wings-like cloak in Rembrandt's painting, I sense the motherly quality of God's love…a love that existed before any rejection was possible and that will still be there after all rejections have taken place. It is the first and everlasting love of a God who is Father as well as Mother. It is the fountain of all true human love, even the most limited. Jesus' whole life and preaching had only one aim: to reveal this inexhaustible, unlimited motherly and fatherly love of his God and to show the way to let that love guide every part of our daily lives.[11]

As we gather at this assembly, an essential task here and at our home congregations is to let that unlimited motherly and fatherly love of God guide every part of our daily lives. As we gather at this assembly, we are a little worse for the wear of this year's storms. The branch holding the nest of our church has taken a beating by the elements—yet the grace of the elements of bread and wine is far greater. We are all like the prodigal son returning home after we have strayed so far from the love intended to guide us and feed us. We need those wings to embrace us; we need refuge; we need a safe, dry place to regroup.

A recent *New York Times* carried a front-page article entitled, "Houses of Worship Struggle to Rebuild After Flood." Dateline: Grand Forks, North Dakota. The lead in: "At the First Presbyterian Church here, last month's flood ruined interior walls and left green and purple song books stuck to ceiling beams in the basement choir room."[12] I couldn't help but think of that as a metaphor for the larger church as well. But by God's grace, our interior walls have not been ruined. By God's grace our interior walls can be reinforced through spiritual nurture and honest, accepting community with one another. Without that, the infrastructure will collapse. In the *Times* article, Carole Peterson, the spiritual director at the Grand Forks church, is quoted as saying, "It has been overwhelming. The church is our home, and if we can't go home, where do we go?"

Where do we go? Where *do* we go? Home, like the prodigal son, to the love that existed before any rejection was possible. Home to the one place where our open, crying mouths can be fed with a mother's love. Home to the nest where no one is shoved. May the world always see us as such a place.

A few weeks ago we found a fledgling soul in our church nursery. A sweet-faced baby girl, who had been abruptly dropped off in the middle of worship, the mother dashing out before any questions could be asked or registration recorded. An hour after worship, long after everyone else had gone home, the mother had not returned. We finally and reluctantly called the police, believing the child to be abandoned. The mother and the police arrived within seconds of each other. We experienced a mix of relief and awkwardness and a certain amount of judgment.

"Your child is just too precious to be left somewhere without information" I scolded her. "She needs you to be responsible." Breathlessly and earnestly the mother pleaded, "I just *had* to go to a job interview. I just had to. I tried to think of the safest place I could leave her." Ah. The safest place. The bird's nest. Shelter, nurture, spiritual fellowship. We Presbyterians can't be the only birds in the nest. What will we do to provide help for those trying to get off welfare who need childcare and bus fare in order to get to the interview? How will we protect the wounded birds of society? God's covenant intends for us all to soar. Every wounded bird is an indictment, every wounded bird holds everyone else back from reaching the heights fully intended.

It seems overwhelming, unless we imagine the wings of God carrying us. Then, like the people in the flooded First Presbyterian Church in Grand Forks, we start peeling the ruined songbooks off the ceiling, one by one, trusting the mother bird to give us new notes to sing, trusting that we are not a solo act, but God's chorus—tuned to God's orchestration. In the book *How the Irish Saved Civilization,* Thomas Cahill wrote:

> No human group has ever figured out how to design its future.
> That future may be germinating today not in a boardroom

in London or an office in Washington or a bank in Tokyo, but in some antic outpost or other—a kindly British orphanage in the grim foothills of Peru, a house for the dying in a back street of Calcutta run by a fiercely single-minded Albanian nun, an easygoing French medical team at the starving edge of the Sahel, a mission to Somalia by Irish social workers who remember their own Great Hunger, a nursery program to assist convict-mothers at a New York Prison—in some unheralded corner where a great-hearted human being is committed to loving outcasts in an extraordinary way.[13]

Sister Joan Chittister tells the story of a traveler who found a small bird lying upside down on its back. "Bird," the traveler said, "Why are you lying upside down like that?" "I heard the heavens are going to fall today," the bird replied. "I suppose," the traveler laughed, "You think your spindly little legs are going to hold it up." And the little sparrow said quietly, "Well, Sir, one does what one can."[14]

And so we shall and so we must do what we can. Person by person, congregation by congregation, governing body by governing body— we must do what we can to provide the shelter, nurture, and spiritual fellowship of all God's children. That is the shelled promise we tend in this nest. Let Jesus gather us under his loving, inclusive, compassionate wings, as he so longs to do. Feel the warmth of that inexhaustible love, remembering that the church, the body of Christ, is our home, and "if we can't go home, where do we go?" The church is called to be a bird's nest, not a hornet's nest. A place we come to be fed, not stung. Because of God's covenant of care, we can fly, and we can use the nest to teach others to fly. God will bear us up on eagles' wings. The unlimited parental love of God allows us to soar as never before, and the fewer wounded birds we leave behind, the higher we'll go. Amen.

CHAPTER 8

Barbara K. *Lundblad*

I'd like to invite you into my kitchen for a cup of coffee, but since my kitchen is too small, let's go across the street to Sakura Park. We can sit on a bench and talk. Well, I'll talk and you can listen, but I hope you'll be talking back as I go along. I must tell you that I've wrestled with a question concerning this assignment: Should I tell you how I actually prepare a sermon, or how I wish I prepared a sermon? I'll go with reality, though I may flag some places that need improvement. I wish we could be talking face-to-face, but even though that's not possible, I'm thinking of this as a conversation. That's how I think about preaching; it's a conversation, even if one person is doing most of the talking. I think of people in the congregation as my preaching partners. They're with me as I hear the text, discern the focus, shape the sermon, and in the moment of preaching. I see questions in their faces, hear their laughter, sense their confusion, and enter the silences between us.

119

Hear that screech? That's the number 1 train stopping at 125th Street a few blocks over. The subway comes up out of the ground at that stop—out of the darkness of the tunnel into the light of day. I'm always surprised, though it happens every time I ride that train. This park bench is a good place to work on sermons because it's full of distractions—like the sound of that train, kids in the sandbox, couples talking up close, bells sounding the hour at Riverside Church, skateboarders over at Grant's Tomb. Distractions are the stuff of everyday life bumping into scripture texts. I always do at least some of my sermon work in the midst of distractions.

Maybe distractions are really encounters—like the one Moses had on the hillside while tending his father-in-law's sheep. Was the burning bush a distraction? That Exodus text has been important for me as I think about preaching: "When the LORD saw that [Moses] had turned aside to see, God called to him out of the bush…" (Ex. 3:4). No doubt God would have found another way to get through, but it's also clear that God didn't speak until Moses turned aside. What would preaching mean if nobody turned aside? In recent years I've found a second text that helps describe my sermon process, a text from Toni Morrison's novel *Beloved*. Do you know the scene in the Clearing? Baby Suggs, the holy woman, is gathering her people—all of them former slaves—in that hidden, sacred space. She sits down on a big, flat-sided rock and prays. Before she speaks anything resembling a sermon, she wants to hear the people. She calls on the children to laugh and the grown men to dance. She calls on the women to cry "for the living and the dead." "It started that way: laughing children, dancing men, crying women and then it got mixed up. Women stopped crying and danced; men sat down and cried; children danced, women laughed, children cried…In the silence that followed, Baby Suggs, holy, offered up to them her great big heart."[1]

That's what a sermon is for me: It's a meeting place between the scripture text and the community text. It's holy ground, where people turn aside to hear God's word passed down over centuries, yet new in this time and place. It's the Clearing where the preacher has listened attentively to the men, women, and children called the congregation. This listening takes place before the preacher says a word.

So when I begin working on a sermon, I have before me a simple chart. Sometimes it's in my head, but I often write it down so I won't forget:

SCRIPTURE TEXT $\longrightarrow$ *MEETING PLACE* $\longleftarrow$ COMMUNITY TEXT

There's an arrow pointing from the Scripture Text to the Meeting Place and another pointing back from the Community Text to the Meeting Place. It's in the Meeting Place where the sermon takes shape. But that meeting can't happen until both "texts" are heard and honored.

Early in the week, Sunday evening or Monday morning, I read the scripture text, or rather, texts. As a Lutheran pastor, I'm guided by the lectionary. So I read three lessons plus the psalm. I don't do anything except listen and pray. Most of the time I move toward the gospel, but not always. In Advent Year A, I often go with Isaiah. These texts offer wondrous pictures for preaching and visual images to enliven the worship space—a shoot growing from a stump, waters flowing in the desert, crocuses blooming, and so forth. The long season of ordinary time might entice me outside the lectionary for a series of sermons on "Forgotten Texts, Neglected Stories" or a topical series on "Family."

If you're not a lectionary preacher, you probably have other ways of choosing the text. If you are a lectionary preacher, you know that much of the First Testament is neglected in the lectionary cycle. You might want to set aside time to preach a series of sermons from the First Testament: the human foibles of our Genesis ancestors, the surprising presence of outsiders such as Rahab and Ruth, the making and undoing of kings, and so forth.

But back to the lectionary. We could walk for a while instead of just sitting here. After I've read all the appointed texts, here's the question: Do I preach on one or all of them? I find it almost impossible to preach on more than one, though I know others who find ways to weave them together. I've learned a few things over the years that guide me in choosing the text:

1. If one of the texts is particularly problematic or if traditional interpretations have been harmful, I'll preach on that text. The sacrifice of Isaac, Jesus' teaching about divorce, the call to bear our cross, the Ephesians text about wives obeying their husbands— those texts can't be read aloud and left hanging.

2. If I hear the community leaning toward one of the texts, I'll move there too. Many people in the congregation feel like the older brother in the parable of the prodigal son, so when Luke 15 comes along, I'll try to find a way to get them to come in and join the party.

3. If something has happened in the community that cries for attention, I try to respond: for example, the Oklahoma City bombing or the killing of Amadou Diallo in New York City. Sometimes the appointed texts don't provide a meeting place. When this happens, I pray for another word from God and set the lectionary aside for that Sunday.

Once I've decided on the primary text, I get to know that passage more intimately. Sometimes, I ask someone else to read the text aloud to me. I want to hear it as people will hear it on Sunday—once through without stopping. If I were in the parish now, I'd try to be more consistent about this. I'd ask a different person to be my "reader" each week—which would mean about fifty people over a year's time who would be my partners in particular ways. Whether I'm listening to the text or reading it, I respond immediately in writing. I start with anything that jumps out: a word, a phrase, a picture, a memory— and I write. I write for twenty minutes without stopping or censoring. (I'm grateful to Anne Lamott's book *Bird by Bird* for encouraging this seemingly aimless writing!) This writing may never enter the pulpit, but it moves me to a place I wouldn't have gone without the freedom to get nowhere at all.

I carry the text with me wherever I go, here to the park or on the subway. On Tuesday or Wednesday, I try to carve out a block of time to enter the text more deeply. This is the hard part for me: writing in my red minister's desk calendar, "Tuesday, 9:00 a.m.—Meeting with S.T." (that is, Sermon Text). When someone asks, "Can you meet on

Tuesday morning?" I'll check my book and say, "No, I have a meeting then." Don't let me fool you—I still don't do this consistently. But I know that if I don't write this on my calendar, my preparation time will be eaten up by things that are written on my calendar and by the emergencies that aren't. At least now I'm trying to reserve a block of time to meet with "S.T." before the week is gone.

I usually do this work in my study—I want privacy so I can move around the room as I read the text aloud. What does my body want to do? When does my body stop or jump or dance or fall down? I check several translations, taking note of differences. I do my best to read the original language with help from an interlinear Bible and other resources. I try to read the words as though I've never heard them before. You know that this is almost impossible after years of seminary and several years of preaching, but it's always worthwhile. I read from a Bible that's not underlined or filled with my notes. Then I jot down questions, especially naïve questions, and pay attention to anything that's odd: a detail that seems superfluous, a reference to something that's gone before ("After six days..."), a perplexing problem, or something that makes me want to argue.

Let's take a break here and go inside for a cup of coffee. This is where I take a break in the sermon process. Before doing any more work with the scripture text, I move to the community text. I used to do this much later, after I'd written most of the sermon. Then I'd ask, "How can I make my sermon relevant to the congregation?" But that was too late! After a few years of preaching, I began to listen to the community text earlier—before I'd done all my own work. It's not a matter of relevance but of discerning the meaning of the scripture text alongside the community text. I want people's questions and concerns to guide my deeper engagement with the text, my search for stories and images and decisions about sermon form.

So I leave my scribbled notes behind and try to listen to voices in the congregation. Sometimes I'm very deliberate in picturing three or four people. I might imagine my way through the church directory from Abbott to Zimmerman. How will Michael and Ruth hear this text? What questions will Leslie and Ben have? What will make them angry? Where will they disagree? What's going on in their lives right now that connects with this text? Has something happened within the whole congregation or in the larger community that changes how this text is heard? I write down all these responses: the anger, the questions, the hope, the despair, the crises, and the laughter.

It's even better if you can go beyond imagining the voices to actually hearing a few. In the parish I met with members each week for text study at an Indian restaurant near the church. Sometimes there were three of us, sometimes twelve. It wasn't so much a teaching session as a conversation with the Sunday texts. I heard the text in a new way as I listened to others. Someone noticed something I'd never seen; someone was confused about something I'd assumed was absolutely clear. Now I'd be more intentional about inviting different people over a year's time: a group of students during Advent, retired people who could meet over lunch during Lent, new members who might stay for Sunday brunch after Easter. You might be thinking—who has time for this? I know how limited time is for parish pastors—if I had time for only one text study group each week, I'd choose to meet with a group of lay members rather than other clergy. If you have time for both, that's great!

Oh, I wanted to tell you some things I won't do. I won't read someone else's sermon on this text—even a preacher whose sermons I dearly love. If I do, I'll either copy that sermon or argue against it, rather than engaging the text anew. I'll try hard not to go to my files to see what I said three years ago when this text came around. This is a different time. I'm different and the community is different (even if it's the same parish and the text hasn't changed). I'll also hold off consulting commentaries until I've done more work with the text myself. I don't want experts to silence my odd questions prematurely or wrap up the loose ends too neatly.

Now I gather up my own responses (free-form writing, naïve questions, odd details, and perhaps a few intuitive insights) along with voices from the community, real or imagined. I'll go back to the scripture text guided by the voices from the community. What precedes this passage and what follows? Do I remember connections to other places in this book—wasn't there something back in chapter two? I try not to jump from one gospel to another but to listen to the particular perspective of Matthew or Mark, Luke or John. I'll check for parallels if there are any: Why does Mark say the heavens were "torn apart" at Jesus' baptism? Of course, these methods will differ from one text to another. An ancestor story in Genesis has a different shape and purpose than Paul's letter to the Romans. Hopefully we can shake loose memories of biblical courses in seminary. Hopefully we've also learned a thing or two since graduation! The discipline of biblical studies has opened our eyes to an array of options for engaging texts.

But I don't want to be so overwhelmed with historical/critical lenses that I miss the words of the text before me. During this past year, my colleague at Union Theological Seminary, Brigitte Kahl, professor of New Testament, has taught me to pay closer attention to the texture of the text, to feel the shape of words and to look for patterns woven in the fabric of the entire book. She encourages students to "feed" a particular passage with information from other parts of that gospel. If the text is the end of Matthew 13, where Jesus returns to his hometown, I pick up some words and hold them in my hand: "the carpenter's son...his mother called Mary...his brothers...his sisters." What feeds these family words? If memory fails me, a concordance will help. How did Jesus' family get started in chapters one and two? How is Jesus' sense of family different from that of his hometown? from Herod's family gathered for their ghastly dinner? Focusing on one gospel for a year is a gift of the lectionary. Patterns become discernible, themes reappear, contrasts become apparent. Preacher and people are once again immersed in the peculiar perspective of one evangelist.

Now I pray in more specific ways for discernment: How is the scripture text meeting the community text this week? What theme or focus is emerging in the Meeting Place? I begin to hear a particular word breaking through for this sermon. This focus directs further exegetical work: What words need deeper study in the original language? What customs or traditions are obscure and need explication? Where do I sense resistance? How can I move into it and through it? At this point I often turn to the commentaries for help with something difficult or to check my intuitive responses. (I try to check three or four different writers, including *The Women's Bible Commentary*.)[2]

By Thursday or Friday—I wish I could say sooner—the focus for this sermon becomes clear. I've discovered over the years that every text opens up more possibilities than one sermon can hold. One of the most difficult tasks of preaching is to leave great ideas behind, tossing them gently into the scrap bag for another sermon. Once I've discerned a primary focus for this sermon, I try to see the shape. Sometimes the shape follows the shape of the scripture text—a biblical narrative retold conversing with the community text, a biblical image reflected in city streets, a parable at the playground. The shape determines how the sermon moves: straight ahead in linear fashion, weaving back and forth between biblical text and community text, going around and around to look at an image from different angles. Sometimes I paint three pictures, trying to touch people in different life situations. Sometimes I hear a refrain or a question that returns again and again, tying the sermon together. Sometimes the end is clear as I begin, but often the ending emerges only in the process of writing. (My computer is filled with unended sermons, their endings scratched out later in pen or in the moment of preaching.)

With the focus and the shape in mind, I start scripting the sermon. I say "scripting" because I want the sermon to be oral rather than written. I often talk aloud as I write. This scripting has been going on all week in some form: my initial free-form writing, my naïve questions, and my notes from the Indian restaurant. I've taken a notebook with me everywhere. I write things down so I'll remember things I'm sure I'll never forget! One subway ride is worth twenty books of "Sure-Fire Sermon Illustrations." The script begins to flow onto either the computer screen or a piece of paper. The computer has made scripting much easier—I can move paragraphs around, change the introduction, pare down repetitions, and print in a sixteen-point font!

Some pieces of the sermon come directly from the scripture text, other pieces from the community's responses, heard or imagined. The script is filled in from other sources as well. I trust stories and images from everyday life most of all. But I also visit writers of novels and short stories or essayists and seers such as Annie Dillard and Joseph Sittler. More and more I read poetry—not to quote poems in sermons (though sometimes I do), but to listen to how poets speak and where they find metaphors. I don't have an orderly system to retrieve writings, but I've learned one helpful trick: I jot key words and page numbers on the blank pages at the back of books. (It's harder if the book is from the library!) If I remember who said it, I can usually find it by checking the back page.

No matter what shape the sermon takes, transitions are crucial. Years ago I got some advice from a parishioner who told me he couldn't always follow where I was going. He took a piece of paper and folded it in half like a church bulletin. "Try typing your sermon on these four half sheets," he said. "No more—then you can work on transitions." That won't be much of a sermon, I thought to myself! But it was wonderful advice. With less material I could pay attention to how pieces were tied together. I could remember more, and I could pause without fear of going on too long.

As I type the script I find the words starting to enter my cells, as if my fingers remember and transfer that memory to my brain. I know this doesn't work for everyone; I also know it works for me after twenty years of preaching better than it did for my first sermon. When the script is printed out—large type, wide margins—I talk it through, underlining and circling words as I go. I often write one-word cues in the margins for quick reference. I leave *big* spaces for pauses or make slash marks to say, "Wait!"

I'd like to tell you that on Sunday morning I spend time quietly, praying and reading through my script one last time. But in the parish I was often teaching the adult class or leading Sunday school worship, dashing into the sacristy at five minutes to 11:00. I'd throw on my alb, search for the acolyte, and put a new wick in the candlelighter. This is not ideal, but it was common. No matter how late, we took time to pray—the acolyte with robe askew, the assisting minister, and I, hands joined, praying for God's Spirit to rest upon us and upon all who gathered.

The opening hymn carries us all into the Clearing. The words of the Kyrie bear my prayer aloft, "For this holy house and for all who offer here their worship and praise, let us pray to the Lord." Before preaching I pray once more in silence. If I'm in a strange place filled with people I don't know, I often invite everyone to sing "Spirit of the Living God"—reminding them that it's not only a prayer for the preacher but a prayer for the Spirit to fall afresh on all of us. Before saying a word, I take in the space and the people, including the choir behind me. I breathe deeply, and the words come off the page. I make sure I know the beginning well—this is not the time to be looking down! These are my partners, and we need to be together from the beginning. After many years of preaching and greater trust in the Spirit's presence, the words come to me—not always as they're printed on the page, but they come. Sometimes I leave the script behind and move out closer to the congregation, without the barrier of the pulpit between us. My body seems to know what to do by now, though that wasn't always true. I'm careful not to wander aimlessly; rather, I trust that movement will come from the words. Sometimes movement helps me remember: I move to the Jordan, then toward the wilderness. I move to the table or the font. I'm careful not to move too close to people, respecting their need for some distance.

One of the most important times with my partners is the pause. This is the silent space in which people answer a question I've asked or think about something in their own lives or prepare for the next move in the sermon. Pausing also opens a space for me to find the next sentence if I've lost my place! Did you ever sing the "Hallelujah Chorus"? Then you probably remember what happens at the very end: The Hallelujahs are repeated over and over until suddenly, there's nothing but silence. That silence takes your breath away and gathers up the meaning of the words. A pause in the sermon can do that.

How does the sermon end? Once, I hope, not twice or three times. Even if the ending is filled in late, I want to know where I'm headed. I don't say "Finally." (I avoid numbers altogether, because people will be counting through the sermon, waiting for "Thirdly.") The ending depends on the sermon shape and what I hope for my partners. Sometimes it's a celebration, a crescendo of phrases. It might be quiet and reflective, or an unanswered question. The ending can be a surprise, but it's not the time to introduce a big new idea. I no longer end with "Amen"—though I once did. When my speaking is over, I want the sermon to continue in the minds and hearts of my partners. Amen sounds so final, as if everything's been said that could ever be said. It's always my prayer that the Spirit will keep working with the sermon after I sit down.

There's much more to say, but the coffee's gone—and it's probably time to start thinking about the sermon for Sunday. So let me leave you with words from poet Mary Oliver. She's talking about poems, but I think we can borrow her words to talk about sermons: "For poems are not words, after all, but fires for the cold, ropes let down to the lost, something as necessary as bread in the pockets of the hungry. Yes, indeed."[3]

The Context of This Sermon

I've talked about my sermon process, remembering sixteen years as pastor at Our Saviour's Atonement Lutheran Church in New York City. Now when I preach it's usually as a guest, and I miss the partnership that only a parish pastor and people can know. I still try to imagine the voices of the community—even if I don't know them well. The following sermon was preached at The Riverside Church in New York in October 1999, at a service celebrating full communion between Lutheran and Reformed churches in the United States. This would be the first time all four denominations worshiped together in the New York region, though the "official" service had happened a year before in Chicago. The gospel text appointed was the journey to Emmaus in Luke 24. This is a very familiar post-Easter text, and I had preached on it many times in the parish—all those old sermons were echoing around in my head.

But this was a different time and a different congregation. People from all four denominations would be gathered, and I wanted to honor our different traditions. I also knew that it was the sacrament of communion itself that had been so divisive between Reformed and Lutheran churches since the sixteenth century. The bread had divided us! Now we were coming together as one body in Christ, but there were still questions about "real presence" and the meaning of communion. I knew that some Lutherans, especially clergy, still felt that the other partners didn't have a "valid" understanding of the sacrament. There were some people from the Reformed churches who were suspicious of Lutherans.

I wanted to include some voices other than my own Lutheran community in the sermon but didn't want the sermon to be a history lesson. Fortunately, a graduate student at Union introduced me to a wonderful address by John Thomas, the newly elected president of the UCC. I found his text on the UCC Web site, and he became one of my conversation partners. I jotted down the comments and complaints I'd heard during the year since our churches voted on the full-communion agreement. I tried to picture faces of people I thought would be there as well as the festive atmosphere of mass choir, robed clergy, and a diverse gathering of laity who were glad this day had finally come.

As I read and reread the Luke text, I walked on the road, and I stopped at the table. This text offered many possibilities for this particular service. But I kept hearing a child's question: Did they eat the bread? It was, in many ways, a silly question, and I wondered if it bore the weight of such a day! Who knows if they ate the bread, and who cares? But it was that question that framed the sermon for me. It seemed to connect to the issue that had divided our churches for almost five hundred years. So I went with that question. I was encouraged during the reception when many people came up to me with their own answers. "Yes, of course they ate the bread!" or "No, they were too excited!" I always give thanks to God when a sermon keeps going after it's over.

After Emmaus

LUKE 24:13–35

There are many texts echoing around this sanctuary today: scripture texts from Isaiah, 1 Corinthians, and Luke. But that's not all—we're mindful of another text: A Formula of Agreement bringing together faith communities separated for almost five hundred years. We bring the texts of our lives in congregations of the Evangelical Lutheran Church in America, the Presbyterian Church in the USA, Reformed Church in America, and United Church of Christ—in alphabetical order! So many texts: hymnals and histories, schisms and condemnations, words, words, and more words, written and shouted since the Reformation. And we have the text of this liturgy first used at Rockefeller Chapel in Chicago a year ago. Dr. Forbes, I guess we could call Riverside Church a different "Rockefeller chapel"!

All these texts move in and out together, a humming continuo under words spoken one at a time. Surrounded by these many texts, I turn to today's gospel reading from Luke chapter 24, and I ask you this simple question: Did they eat the bread?

I mean Cleopas and the unnamed disciple sitting at the table in Emmaus. The text says, "When he was at the table with them, he took bread, blessed and broke it, and gave it to them. Then their eyes were opened, and they recognized him; and he vanished from their sight." The stranger was no longer a stranger—they knew he was Jesus. But it doesn't tell whether they ate the bread.

Would you have eaten the bread, or would you have saved it? I would have wanted to save it, to hold it carefully without losing a crumb. I would have carried it back to Jerusalem to show the others: "Look! We have seen the Lord! He broke bread and gave it to us!" But what sort of testimony would that be? The bread would look like ordinary bread from the baker's. That bread wouldn't have proved a thing.

It's a silly question, isn't it? That wasn't the heart of the story. This story moves toward the table, walks on the road toward that moment captured as if in a ray of pure light. The one they knew only as a stranger, broke bread, and gave it to them—and their eyes were opened. He was no longer a stranger, but the risen Lord. We don't need to know if they ate the bread there and then or on the road back to Jerusalem, or if they kept it in their hands. The risen Jesus had come to stay with them forever.

It was a silly question, wasn't it? And yet we've been asking questions about the bread for centuries. Is Christ present in it? If so, how? Does the bread become something other than bread? Can we eat bread with those who don't believe what we believe about the bread? It is here at this table where bread is broken that our churches have been most broken. We have gone on Crop Walks together, sponsored food pantries and shelters, joined in ecumenical Thanksgiving services—but we have not come to the table together, except in secret.

Now, after years of walking on that long and often difficult road called "Lutheran-Reformed Dialogues"—or "Reformed-Lutheran Dialogues"—our churches have reached an agreement called "full communion," saying: Both Lutheran and Reformed churches affirm that Christ himself is host at the table. Both churches affirm that Christ himself is truly present and received in the supper. Neither communion professes to explain how this is so.[4]

"But"—no buts! We need to put an end to all of our I-know-a-minister stories. As in "I know a Lutheran pastor who kneels down as though worshiping the bread and wine!" or "I know a Presbyterian minister who called communion a symbol," or "I know a UCC minister who…" or "I went to an RCA church and they…" You can fill in the blanks. If we're honest, we know that there are people within our own denominations with whom we disagree on almost everything!

Sisters and brothers, this agreement doesn't mean that we are the same. Our liturgies still sing and speak different words. We receive the bread and cup in different ways. But today we proclaim that the One who broke bread at Emmaus gathers up our differences and invites us to eat together at this one table. Our eyes have been opened: In the presence of Jesus we are no longer strangers.

So is that the end of our journey? It wasn't the end for the two who sat at Emmaus with pieces of broken bread in their hands. Oh, I think they ate the bread then and there—with uninhibited delight!

Then they got up and ran off, filled with bread and with resurrection. They ran back to the city they had fled. At that very hour they returned to Jerusalem, though by then it must have been dark. News of life and hope couldn't wait until morning. Their lives had been transformed at the table.

What about our lives? Are we transformed at this table? What does the real presence of Christ mean for us? Here I turn to another text, words written by Rev. John Thomas, newly elected President of the United Church of Christ. Since a Lutheran was invited to preach, it seemed only fair to let someone from the Reformed family also get a word in. In an address given last year, Rev. Thomas urged our churches to continue conversation about the eucharist—even though we may be tempted to drop the subject now that we've voted! He speaks of the eucharist as "a mystical and a moral presence" and suggests some questions to keep the conversation going:

> Does it trouble us that the multiracial, multicultural richness of the messianic vision is often anticipated more fully in our schools and places of business than it is in our churches when we gather for the "feast of the kingdom"?

> When the groaning tables of the north are isolated from the nearly barren tables of the south, or when the railroad tracks separate rich and poor not only at work and play, but also at Table, can we truly believe our Eucharist has the power to renew the creation in the image of God's new age?[5]

We're invited to come to Christ's table as we are, but that doesn't mean we'll leave unchanged—for the eucharist is a mystical and a moral presence, a sustaining and subversive power. Several years ago my friend Jon Nelson, a Lutheran pastor in Seattle, was arrested for protesting the deployment of Trident submarines. Jon and others were particularly outraged when one of the nuclear submarines was christened USS Corpus Christi, named for the city in Texas but meaning the body of Christ. Jon joined others in their little speedboats to stop the Trident from entering Puget Sound. Of course the powerful Trident wasn't stopped, and Jon was arrested. While he was in jail, several friends came to visit. One of the pastors in the group brought a loaf of bread and a plastic container of wine—they knew a wine bottle would never be allowed. But prison authorities confiscated the wine and the bread as contraband. Jon's friends were dismayed, for they so wanted to share communion with him in prison. But when they told him what had happened, Jon broke into an enormous grin. "Communion as contraband! That's it, isn't it?" he said. "Communion as contraband—threatening to the powers who think they own the world." The eucharist is a moral and mystical presence, a subversive and sustaining presence.

"Stay with us," they said as they neared Emmaus. The narrator slows down now, repeating words and phrases. "'Stay with us'…So he went in to stay with them." Strange isn't it? Jesus stayed with them by leaving. So much is strange about this familiar story. Isn't it odd that two unknown disciples carry this wondrous Easter gospel? The first communion of the resurrection is shared with two people we've never heard of—why not Peter or John or Mary Magdalene? Cleopas appears nowhere else in scripture, and his companion isn't named at all. Some say it was a woman, maybe Cleopas' wife. I don't know. Did Luke know? I wonder…perhaps Luke left out the name on purpose, a blank space for you and me to fill in our own names.

"Stay with us," they said. He took the bread, blessed it and broke it, and gave it to them. Their eyes were opened, and he vanished, leaving them with pieces of broken bread and each other. Soon, we will join them, reaching out our hands. We'll be standing here with pieces of broken bread and each other. "This is my body, which is given for you." Strange, isn't it? Those words weren't spoken at Emmaus, and yet their eyes were opened. We'll hear those words today. Jesus Christ truly present, gathering up all our differences. "This is my body," Jesus says, stretching out his arms to embrace everyone in this sanctuary.

One of those who received the bread was named Cleopas.

And the other?

You know. Come and eat.

CHAPTER 9

Karen Stokes

First off, I have a confession to make. It has to do with the sin of pride, and how it goeth before a fall. Last summer I was invited to come back and preach at the seminary where I'd received my theological education. This was one of those *big deal* invitations. I was being asked to deliver the sermon at one of two services of worship held during the big annual endowed lecture series. A prestigious keynote speaker is brought in to give three lectures on an important topic within his or her discipline, and the lectures (and chapel services) are attended by alumni/ae, trustees, students, faculty, prospective students, and other church folk from around the area.

I admit that I jumped at the opportunity. I was right in the middle of D.Min. classes at the seminary, with an emphasis on preaching, and I was feeling good about the progress I'd made as a preacher in my sixteen years of ordained ministry. I had visions in my head of the thrill it would be to strut my homiletical stuff before such a distinguished congregation, and I began to imagine the sermon I would deliver: a sermon that would strike the perfect balance between heart and mind, a sermon that would be folksy yet profound, exegetically sound, pastorally sensitive, and prophetically compelling. In short, I imagined preaching a sermon reminiscent in both style and content of the work of my favorite preacher, Dr. James Forbes of the Riverside Church in New York City. If I could be any preacher in the world, it would be Dr. Forbes. Every time I hear him, in person or on videotape, I am simply astonished by his mastery of the art and science of preaching. I am moved, without fail; and I am humbled by the realization of how much I have yet to learn as a preacher.

But this invitation from the seminary made me think that perhaps I was moving up in the homiletical world. I was recognized. I was gaining a reputation. I was feeling dangerously proud of myself…

A few days after accepting the invitation, I dropped by the dean's office to find out what was known at this early date about the keynote speaker, at least what area of expertise the person came from—New Testament, Old Testament, Theology—so I could start to think about tying my sermon thematically to the topic of the lectures. Did they know yet who the keynoter was going to be?

"It's going to be Dr. James Forbes of the Riverside Church in New York City."

Oh. Very funny, God. I guess I get your point.

If I could be any preacher in the world, Dr. Forbes would top my list. However, as that experience in the dean's office so graphically reminded me, there is only one preacher I can be, and that is Karen Stokes. This fact is the key to my creative process as I write sermons.

Phillips Brooks said, "Preaching is truth through personality."[1] To me, this means that my job as a preacher is to bring everything that I am—my experience, my education, my perspective, my strength, my weakness—to the weekly task of preaching. Many other voices inform and shape what I say on Sunday morning; but, appropriately enough, given our faith's unique emphasis on incarnation, God funnels God's great, redemptive, transforming truth to and through us as individual human beings. So when I create a sermon, my primary goal is to tell the truth and to move my congregation to their own experiences of that truth. At each stage of sermon writing, from the initial brainstorming to the final version, I ask three things: Do I mean it? Do I believe it? and Is it faithful to the gospel?

Having said all that, let me take some time to lay out the specifics of my sermon-writing process. I won't say that this is my "normal" process, because every week is unique (and uniquely uncontrollable), but this is what I aim for. I work with a liturgical team at my church. This team is composed of the associate pastor, the children's education director, the music director, the organist, and me. We meet about once a month to plan the services for the weeks ahead. We choose hymns, decide what the "Children's Time" is going to involve, work out the logistics of special events such as communion and baptism, and so on. In order for me to be ready for this meeting, I have to have some sense of what the general theme of each sermon will be.

First, I read the lectionary passages. The church I currently serve does not have a tradition of following the lectionary, but just for my own discipline I like to start there. If I am alone when I'm working (whether at home or at the office), I like to read each passage aloud a couple of times. I quickly jot down a few thoughts about each passage—a question it might raise, a word or phrase that catches my attention—after which I do the same for the other passages for that week and the weeks following. Then I just let them percolate for a while.

Second, I don't stop with the lectionary. My congregation is very justice-oriented and actively engaged in the world, and they want to hear what the preacher has to say about the issues of the day. This, of course, is fraught with peril for that preacher. The temptation toward proof-texting is subtle and insidious, even when I think I'm being careful. The best warning I've heard that keeps me from resorting to proof-texting when writing a topical sermon is: Don't use the Bible the way a drunk uses a lamppost—more for support than for illumination.

Instead, I try to read up on the issue at hand, in newspapers, magazines, religious and secular journals, in order to grasp the central underlying question. I think of it as the *big issue*. What's the big issue at the heart of a particular contemporary crisis? Is it power, greed, materialism? The need for worldly recognition or worldly security? Is it the fear of loss, the fear of death? All of these are theological questions, and I as preacher believe that it is my job to reflect on them theologically. So I don't look for passages of scripture that prove my own political point of view; instead, I look for passages that will inform my (and the congregation's) reflection on those same theological questions.

There is also a third option I exercise in choosing my theme for a given Sunday. Last summer I tried something new, which I called "Preaching by Request." In the spring, through the Sunday bulletin and the weekly newsletter, I invited people to suggest sermon topics, anything they'd like to have me talk about on a Sunday morning. The response was wonderful. They didn't pick small topics, either. They suggested things like "God," "Heaven," "Forgiveness." It was a great way for me, having been at this church for only about a year, to hear what their big issues were, and it was a great way for the people in the church to know what kinds of questions their friends were raising. (An unexpected benefit of the series was that attendance stayed strong all summer!)

Choosing the scripture and theme for each week is just the first part of the brainstorming process. Over time I have realized the importance of brainstorming in my sermon-writing enterprise. It is where I spend the largest percentage of my sermon prep time, hands down. I try not to narrow my options any sooner than I must, in order to leave time and space for the creative workings of the Spirit. It has taken me many years to be comfortable with this openness. When it comes to time management, my personal tendency is toward anxiety; that is, I tend to push toward closure and resolution of just about everything as quickly as possible, just so I don't have to worry about it anymore. Sometimes it is helpful, but in terms of sermon writing it can serve to close homiletical doors long before I even realize they are open. Each Sunday is so full of possibility and potential; and if I can let myself live with that potential for a while and not lock myself into a particular homiletical direction too soon, I find that I often go much deeper into the heart of a text than if I just grab the first "preachable" idea that floats by.

Once I have chosen the scripture and the general theme for the coming weeks and the liturgical team has met, I start to work in earnest on the sermon for the next Sunday. This is still brainstorming time, but now I focus on a particular passage. Early in the week, I spend some time reading the passage, slowly, several times over. In a manner of speaking, I pray the scripture, seeking to open myself up to the movement of the Spirit. Again, I find it very helpful to read/

pray it aloud, especially if it's a story that I think I am very familiar with. I'm constantly amazed at the surprises, even the shocks, I have found when reading a "well-known" story. Once, I was choosing readings for a Maundy Thursday service and decided on the first part of Luke 23, Jesus before Pilate and Herod. As the two leaders pass Jesus back and forth, the story grows more dramatic and frightening, and then comes verse 12: "That same day Herod and Pilate became friends with each other; before this they had been enemies." How many times have I read that story and never noticed that incredible statement? So of course, that "unholy alliance" became the central point of exploration in my meditation that evening.

As I read the passage I will be preaching from, I jot lots of notes at random: questions that the scripture raises for me, particular words or lines that resonate, stories or illustrations that come to mind, just about anything that drifts through my consciousness as I let the scripture soak in. This process takes some time, and I usually end up with three to five pages of random ideas. Then I go back and read what I have written, and usually some basic organizing idea begins to come into focus out of the diffuse cloud of questions and associations.

If I'm not too anxious about time, I let that be the total of the first day's active homiletical work. However, I find that once I have started to open myself to a particular passage, the world around me is suddenly filled with connections—an image in a magazine ad, a conversation with a parishioner, a song on the radio—and they all pull me deeper and deeper into an immediate experience of the gospel message. What I'm trying to find through this process is the heart of the scripture passage, which will ultimately become the "point" of the sermon. I want to find that taut cord of truth running through the story that, when plucked on Sunday morning, will set up sympathetic vibrations in the lives and experiences of the people who gather in that place for worship.

Over the next few days, I more systematically begin to invite other people into my ruminations as I exegete the passage. I read commentaries, do word study, and dig through my files for articles, quotes, and anecdotes I may have tucked away thinking that someday they might be useful in a sermon. I talk to other preachers; I talk to the parishioners I see during the week, trying out ideas on them to see what they think and how they respond. I also make use of a wonderful resource, the people who were my teachers in seminary. Some have retired; some are still on the faculty; and none have ever discouraged me when I've called to ask them about whatever I'm working on. None have ever implied that my questions are foolish or that my calls are unwelcome. As before, I take random notes as I read and think and talk, still making no attempt to organize those thoughts into any coherent structure quite yet. Aside from a few hours of focused study, this exegetical work takes place around and within the rest of the work I do each week—administration, pastoral care, committee meetings—you know the drill.

Toward the end of the week, I start trying to tease a sermon out of the great amorphous mass of notes and experiences that have gathered on my desk and in my life during that past few days. By now the direction, or central point, of the sermon has begun to become clear as the random notes and thoughts coalesce in some subconscious way, drawing me closer to that cord of truth. My husband says that his image of my sermon-writing process is me sitting on the bed, a dog or two snoozing next to me, dozens of sheets and scraps of paper fanned out around me, and pen and paper in hand as I begin to turn all this stuff into a sermon.

So now the fun starts. At this point I begin to give serious consideration to form as well as content. This is the part of the preaching task that I most enjoy, because it is where I get to ask the question: How will I best communicate the message of this passage to this community of people on this particular morning?

This is a great era in which to be a preacher. When I attended seminary twenty years ago, the preaching classes still emphasized the classic format for the Presbyterian sermon: Introduction (often a joke or a story), point one, transition, point two, transition, point three, conclusion. People were starting to push the envelope a little bit, but I think we students were mostly trying to get good at the three-point sermon. The left hemisphere of the brain was emphasized. Encouraging any intuitive or emotional connection was risky. Singing was rare, shouting unheard of. We preached from carefully written manuscripts, which were turned in to the instructor for review.

Now, all that has changed. Books on homiletical theory reflect the diversity of voices and styles that are now taken seriously in the field. Women preachers, African American preachers, Third World preachers—all are enriching the homiletical gene pool with their new blood and spirit. Preachers are encouraged to include elements in our sermons that will appeal not only to the listeners' intellects but to their intuitive and emotional selves as well. When I preach on forgiveness, I don't simply want the listeners to understand forgiveness; I want them to experience it. That experience is dictated to some extent by the homiletical options I choose.

So when I write a sermon, I give careful consideration to how the message will best be communicated. Eugene Lowry's rhetorical strategies for "centering" a sermon—using image, story, or argument—are very helpful to me at this stage of the creative process.[2]

Thus, my decision at this point in the creative process is how best to invite the congregation to participate in the experience of this particular biblical passage. For Dr. Lowry, this involves a decision about the orientation of the sermon, informed by:

1. Preacher's natural "voice"
2. Text's fundamental shape
3. Congregation's mode of receptivity
4. Occasion's particular need
5. Message's primary thrust[3]

After considering these five questions, I can begin to make some choices about the rhetorical center of the sermon. Does this message call for a sermon based on a particular image, which engages the intuitive faculties of the listeners as they are invited to "stop and look"[4] at an image or series of images suggested by the text? Will that text be better served by a cogent and well-reasoned argument that engages the listeners in the intellectual pursuit of a truth that lies within the passage? Or does the situation call for a story that invites the listeners to interact with the text, to become a part of the narrative in some way?

I think it is important to make note of Lowry's assertion that all sermons are "narrative" sermons and that there is a difference between narrative and story.

All sermons are narrative in that they involve a plot form, which begins with a felt discrepancy or conflict, and then makes its way through complication (things always get worse), makes a decisively sharp turn or reversal, and then moves finally toward a resolution or closure.[5]

Thus, whether the rhetorical center is image, argument, or story, my goal is that each sermon will have a narrative flow and that the listeners will be engaged on the intuitive, cognitive, and emotive levels. The only distinction is that when I write an image-centered sermon, my primary focus is on the intuitive experience of the listener, whereas an argument focuses primarily on the cognitive and a story on the emotive.

I make use of a wide range of homiletical options within the image/argument/story structure when deciding how best to get the point across. Once, when the text was the Magnificat, I used poems and songs about motherhood and the yearning for justice. Another time, when exploring the story of Shiphrah and Puah, the Hebrew midwives who defied Pharaoh's order to kill the boy babies (Ex. 1:15–22), I switched into the role of a white male businessman, with a wife, grown kids, and certain moral assumptions, who was confused by the way this biblical story seemed to be saying that sometimes God approves of, and even rewards, dishonesty. The only way I indicated that I was now speaking in someone else's voice was that I sat down in a leather executive's chair that I put up near the pulpit and made my gestures, movements, and postures more typically "masculine." Once I worked with my friend Dave Steele and wrote a musical about the healing of the ten lepers, called "Where Are the Other Nine?" and performed it in worship with some folks from the congregation.[6] Obviously, the parameters that used to define "sermon" have broadened considerably!

This leads to a discussion of the options I consider as far as the use of space on Sunday morning. I think this is another important aspect of how a sermon communicates, and I give it careful thought as I write. I wish I had the time and energy to be so prepared on Sunday that I could always preach without notes. As this is not the case, I frequently preach from the pulpit, using a fairly simple outline. Sometimes however, especially if I'm preaching on a particularly difficult or painful topic, I will just sit on a stool with my notes on a music stand in front of me. This simple change of position in the chancel is understood, consciously or unconsciously, by the people in my congregation to mean that I am talking more personally, talking "right to them," as one parishioner said. I use this physical posture to imply that I am not so much "plucking the cord of truth" as I am still struggling to discover the truth myself and inviting the congregation into that conversation. Then there are those lovely Sundays when I do know where I'm going with a sermon and am so clear and confident about my message that I can preach with only a Bible and a few well-placed Post-Its. On those mornings I am free to roam the chancel (and perhaps the center aisle), making direct eye contact and enjoying the immediacy and intimacy of the preaching moment.

All things considered, I am immensely grateful for the chance to preach to a caring, committed, insightful, demanding, and forgiving community of seekers every Sunday morning. The luxury of immersing myself in God's Word every week is one I do my very best to appreciate, even when the week spins out of control and I wish, if only for a moment, that someone else would step into that pulpit for me. When a sermon goes well, when all the creativity, prayer, openness, and study coalesce into a moment of deep and authentic communication, when the good news of the gospel is preached and heard, I am usually far too relieved to slip into the sin of pride.

But allow me to finish the story of my preaching experience at the seminary. The sermon I ended up delivering at San Francisco Theological Seminary during the T. V. Moore lectures in the spring of 2000 is printed below. I had three goals in mind as I wrote: First, I wanted to tie in with Dr. Forbes's topic for the series, "Learning to Speak in Other Tongues: The Challenge of the Church in the 21st Century," his reflections on the diverse ways in which the Spirit speaks to us and through us as preachers; second, knowing that the chapel service would be attended by seminary students and prospective students, I wanted to stretch the definition of "sermon" as far as I could while still remaining faithful to the gospel; and third, I knew I had to speak in the voice authentically my own.

This sermon had its first stirrings of life the summer before, when I was reading an article in *The Atlantic Monthly* referred to on the cover as "Why Your Dog Pretends to Like You."[7] (I live with four dogs and enjoy the study of dog behavior as an avocation.) The gist of this article was that in the past 100 years, as dog breeders have attempted to strengthen and purify specific breeds by careful control of bloodlines, they have unwittingly bred odd genetic flaws into the breeds. As I read, the thought occurred to me that this was a great metaphor for the denomination in which I serve: that we suffer the consequences of inbreeding when we make our theological, doctrinal and liturgical boundaries too rigid. That article went into my "maybe I can use this in a sermon someday" file.

Later that summer, I was in a preaching class with Eugene Lowry as part of my D.Min. program. As he introduced the idea of rhetorical strategies for centering a sermon, he asked us each to pick one passage of scripture and outline three sermons using that text. One sermon was to be image-centered, one story-centered, and one argument-centered.

I chose as my text the story of the Syrophoenician woman, Mark 7:24–30. I have always found this text to be tremendously challenging, especially because of Jesus' use of a racial epithet when he calls the woman and her daughter "dogs." I looked forward to exploring this story in three different homiletical directions, especially with the reassuring freedom of knowing that I would never actually have to preach any of them!

As I did some brainstorming for the "image" sermon, an obvious central image was the dog. I remembered the article on dog genetics, and as I played with the metaphor of inbreeding, I imagined preaching this sermon using several of my dogs as illustrations. (At this point, I was imagining preaching in my own church, where they are used to such things.) I drafted an outline, presented it to the class, and turned it in to Dr. Lowry. He returned it a few days later with the note, "Very creative and effective. My main concern is whether your love and knowledge of dogs might get too long a leash and delay the plot's movement. You wouldn't want the tail to wag the dog!"

However, the congregation at Montclair Presbyterian Church is willing to give me plenty of time to get to the point when I preach, and they seem happy to let a metaphor, story, or argument develop for quite a while before the point emerges. So I gave the "dog sermon" a try as a work-in-progress at Montclair that summer, with very heartening results. The people laughed at all the right places, the dogs behaved themselves, and the point, when it finally emerged from the chaos, received a hearty round of applause.

When I heard what Dr. Forbes's topic for the Moore lectures was going to be, that "dog sermon" came to mind as a real possibility for the chapel service. It fit my criteria, and I was anxious for an opportunity to refine the text of the sermon and try it out again, but

I was concerned about whether or not dogs would be allowed in the chapel! I met with the chaplain of SFTS and explained what I wanted to do, and he graciously agreed to let me bring my canine companions into the great stone chapel at the top of Seminary Hill.

The chapel service was to be held immediately following the second of Dr. Forbes's three lectures. The opening lecture was given the night before, and, with my sermon written and ready to go, I listened carefully and with some trepidation to see if Dr. Forbes and I really were in agreement on the point of his presentation. I was greatly relieved to find that we were (he even talked a bit about DNA!), and I jotted down a few of his comments to work into my conclusion the next day.

A few words about the logistics of the sermon itself: I had my notes on a music stand in the center of the chancel. An easel next to it held the large signs that I displayed at certain points in the sermon. The dogs waited outside the chapel with my husband and another assistant, and each was sent up the aisle at its proper moment. We had practiced their entrances and exits several times before the service, so they would be familiar with the space and with what was expected of them. Obviously, all three of these dogs are good-natured and pretty obedient, which was essential in order for their presence to enhance rather than detract from the gospel message.

Inbreeding

MARK 7:24–30

It's my understanding that the preacher's exegetical task is to learn all that we can about the context of the biblical story—its historical context, its social context, its linguistic, economic, cultural contexts—so that we can have some understanding of the world in which the story we are preaching from was originally told. The homiletical task is then to draw connections between that world and the world of the modern listener who hears our sermons, exploring the similarities and the differences, the points of connection and the points of contrast, in order that modern listeners might hear a message speaking to them out of the ancient text.

As I read this story of the Syrophoenician woman's encounter with Jesus, one obvious difference between her world and ours is a profound increase in the status of dogs. In the Bible, there are no positive references to dogs. They are vicious; they eat all manner of filth; they are worthless and unclean. But these days, things have definitely changed for the better as far as the status of dogs is concerned. They have become the fuzzy little hearts of a multibillion-dollar industry in this country. They have their own Web sites from which they can buy food and toys. They have their own spokes-puppet on TV commercials. They are coming up in the world.

I would suggest that the main reason for their increase in status is this: They have become useful to human beings. I want to talk about that for a few minutes. Specifically, I want to talk about dog genetics. [Place on easel the sign which bears the word *Genetics*.] Please bear with me on this—I promise I will get to the point before the next seminar is scheduled to begin.

At some point in the one hundred thousand–year history of the relationship between humans and dogs, people began the selective breeding of dogs for certain canine attributes—certain behaviors, certain temperament, certain physical characteristics. The attributes they were bred for were ones that would make the dogs helpful in some way as humans struggled to survive in a world full of challenges. They bred dogs for hunting, for herding, as guardians, and as companions. They bred dogs to do a job.

Take herding dogs. [At my signal, Duncan, a handsome and attentive Border Collie, lopes to the chancel and sits next to me.] This is a Border Collie, one of the herding breeds. The purpose of a herding dog is to control stock—to make the herd move when the shepherd wants it to move, and to stay in place when that's what the shepherd wants. Border Collies move stock by intimidation. They have a particular stare that unnerves the sheep and causes them to drift away from its implied threat. This stare is called "eye." Let me demonstrate. [Duncan has been sitting calmly, looking around with mild interest at the congregation and the surroundings. I pull out a small stuffed toy and move it in front of him. He immediately rises to his feet, drops his head into a predatory posture and locks an intense stare on the toy. I move the toy slowly back and forth, and his gaze never wavers. The congregation chuckles, a bit nervously.]

This is "eye." It didn't matter what a herding dog looked like, or who his great-great-grandsire was, as long as he could control sheep. [I flip the toy to Duncan, and he heads back down the aisle to my assistant.]

All this began to change in the mid-nineteenth century. People began breeding dogs as a hobby—no longer for certain behaviors, but for looks. Breed clubs began to form, which set exacting standards for physical conformation. Breeds became more and more distinct and specialized: No longer did you just have a Retriever, now there were Golden Retrievers, Flat-Coated Retrievers, Chesapeake Bay Retrievers, Labrador Retrievers.

Registries were formed. Now this is a key event in dog genetics. Breed clubs decided that in order for one's dog to be registered as a particular breed, you had to be able to trace that dog's parentage back to a small number of ancestors who defined that breed. Those ancestors are called "Founding Sires."

[Sign: *Founding Sires*]

Dogs now were being bred not for ability, but for purity. A dog's value came to be based on its pedigree, its bloodlines. The mixing of breeds was strictly forbidden. The word "mongrelization" came into common usage during this period (and not only in reference to dogs, as I'm sure you know). Because of this new emphasis on the purity of bloodlines, there was no longer the free flow of genetic diversity that had gone on before this time. This careful, selective breeding within the limited genetic range of a particular kind of dog was supposed to strengthen and perfect the breeds, emphasizing their strengths and minimizing their weaknesses. But it backfired. As people bred for perfection, they bred in unanticipated, unpredictable, and even bizarre genetic disasters.

[Sign: *Springer rage*]

Springer Spaniels have been used as bird dogs and family dogs for a long time. They are by nature cheerful, friendly creatures. But just in the past twenty years or so, strange behaviors are showing up in Springers, the most disturbing being unprovoked rage, in which the dog will suddenly, and for no reason, attack—frequently a family member. Some ancient recessive gene has been brought to the fore because of the limited genetic pool, and dog and human are paying the price.

[Sign: *Pointer Phobia*]

Dog behaviorists are starting to report this genetic problem, in which a seemingly normal dog will literally become rigid with fear, again with no apparent cause. Neither behavior modification techniques nor drug therapies have yet been successful in freeing these animals of their terrors.

[Sign: *Merle Deafness*]

As dogs were bred for their looks rather than abilities, color became an important factor in breeding. There is a beautiful color that shows up occasionally in some of the herding breeds, called blue merle—a soft, mottled gray color that is very distinctive. [Up to the chancel comes Spunky, a pretty blue merle Shetland Sheepdog. She sits and smiles graciously at the congregation.] The merle gene is recessive, so the only way you can guarantee merle puppies is to breed two merle parents. Unfortunately, this pairing also carries potential genetic disaster, because the merle gene is also related to deafness. Statistically, about 25 percent of merle-to-merle puppies are born deaf, and they are usually euthanized by the breeder. This disaster can be prevented by breeding a merle dog to one of another color, but unethical breeders prefer the guaranteed return despite the suffering it causes. [Spunky sweeps back down the aisle, pausing to bestow a wag on some members of her adoring public as she goes.]

Perhaps by now you can see my point beginning to emerge. Obviously, I'm not just talking about dogs here, but about inclusivity and exclusivity, diversity and homogeneity. Maybe the point might be even clearer if I tell you that one indication that a merle-to-merle puppy is deaf is that it is "excessively white."

[Sign: The logo of the Presbyterian Church in the USA]

There are some battles going on in the Presbyterian Church, as in other denominations, that have to do with purity. We take purity seriously. When we're ordained, we promise to further the peace, unity, and purity of the church. But the problem is that we can't seem to agree on a definition. What is purity?

We hear the call for a return to theological orthodoxy and traditional doctrine, the implication being that our theology has been "mongrelized" by too many years of cultural relativism and religious pluralism. We hear the call to set clear doctrinal boundaries around the denomination so that we will know who's in and who's out. Perhaps we could purify ourselves by starting a registry, a role of purebred Presbyterians who can trace our theology and practice back to a certain, limited number of founding sires: say, Calvin, Knox, and Barth.

As we fight these battles for denominational purity, I would encourage the church to look to the dog world and to take heed of the disasters that have been suffered there because of inbreeding: Unprovoked rage. Irrational fear. Preventable deafness. The genetic experts in the dog world are working diligently to begin addressing the problems that inbreeding has caused. They say now that the only way to correct these genetic disasters is by the careful reinfusion of genetic diversity, bringing about what is known as:

[Sign: *Mongrel Vigor*]

It is more politely called "hybrid vigor," but I prefer the more earthy terminology. [I call Jordi, a small black dog of obviously indeterminate parentage to come up. He charges up the aisle and straight toward me where I stand in the chancel. He skids to a stop in front of me and shoots straight into the air, overflowing with joie de vivre. As he lands, he whirls a few times in hot pursuit of his tail, and then trots back happily to where I stand.]

Carefully reintroducing outside blood and new genetic material into these deteriorating bloodlines is the only way, geneticists say, to restore health and strength to these creatures. It will require a whole new definition of the word *purity,* but the alternative is clearly a dead end. [Jordi romps back down the aisle.]

It is interesting to me that Jesus calls the Syrophoenician woman a dog. She clearly represents the threat of the mongrelization of the Messianic mission. Her very existence violates the priestly purity code. She is a Gentile, an outsider, insinuating herself into the picture, insisting on a place at the table for herself and her daughter. "It is not fair," Jesus says, "to take the children's food and throw it to the dogs."

Her response is nothing less than earthshaking, and its echoes still shake the foundations of the church as we struggle for new definitions of purity. She introduces the fresh voice of the outsider, with her quick intelligence, her insistence on compassion, her humor, her new perspective. "But she answered him, 'Sir, even the dogs under the table eat the children's crumbs.'" And apparently she speaks the truth, for Jesus heals her daughter. The Syrophoenician woman's insistence on inclusion does not threaten Jesus' mission with impurity; rather, she strengthens and expands its horizon with fresh new vision.

The poet Carl Sandburg was once asked what was the ugliest word in the English language. His answer: *exclusive*. It is easy in the church to confuse purity with exclusivity, and when we do so, we continue to threaten the church with the dis-ease and vulnerability of inbreeding. Exclusivity is an impurity in the church. So are rage, fear, and deafness.

I would assert that what the church needs now is a good infusion of mongrel vigor. We can get that by listening to those who are speaking in other tongues, those who lurk under the metaphorical table, rather than hearing only those who are sitting at the table as the legitimate children of the founding sires.

I pray that we will have the courage to listen to the voices of those "others" out there—scientists and economists, feminists and womanists, voices out of the Third World, voices out of the gay and lesbian communities. Dr. Forbes spoke last night about those "others" when he said, "Perhaps God draws us into relationship with those others in order to help us get started in dealing with the Wholly Other." The voice of the outsider can speak the word of God, and it is at our peril that we refuse to listen to those voices. Dr. Forbes called us to the same courageous attitude as this scripture does, to that "abhorrence for the facile denial of the authenticity in others." To be truly open to the movement of the Spirit in our world, we must abhor the facile denial of the authenticity in others.

The church is not purified by inbreeding. The church is purified by opening up to the cleansing, invigorating power of the Holy Spirit. If we can truly trust in that Spirit, if we dare find our security in that which we cannot control, that which forces us to move beyond our own comfort zone, then perhaps by the grace of God we can risk hearing the truth, even when it's spoken in tongues. Amen.

CHAPTER 10

Barbara Brown *Taylor*

It is always a challenge for me to compose a sermon, but since there is almost nothing I would rather do, I won't call it "hard." When I am working on a sermon, I fall into a state of what creative theorists call "flow." I forget what time it is. I forget to eat. I forget all the other things that I was absolutely supposed to do today, and I emerge from the process with more energy than I went into it with. Here is how it feels, almost every time: Dive into the water, briefly panic, splash around, get my bearings, then swim and float for the next four to six hours, emerging from the water exhausted and happy.

My process is not something I am in control of; I am just a willing participant in it. It is subject to everything from the weather to my own physical health. Once I am in the water, I never know what will brush up against me or what I will find if I put my feet down on the bottom. The predictable ups and downs have to do with how well I am managing the rest of my time. If I leave too little time for a sermon, then I am almost guaranteed a "down." In my experience, sermons don't like being given last priority. They do not respond well to that. But when I protect enough time to honor the process, I can usually count on an "up."

The Pattern

I start by turning the ringers off on all of my telephones, closing the door to my room, and sitting down with all my books and a cup of hot tea. If I can persuade my Jack Russell terrier to sit in my lap, then all the better. I work in a reclining chair with a bookshelf to my right and a reading stand to my left. It is the most comfortable and comforting place in my house. I feel about it the way a Zen student must feel about her black cushion. It is the place I sit when I want to give myself to one thing. Just sitting there primes the pump for me.

Surroundings are extremely important to me. I do not work well in the midst of domestic chaos. I am one of those people who needs to clean her room before she can do decent work. By my chair, I keep a small, hand-painted icon of the Trinity I found in Ethiopia. On the wall opposite me are a pair of drawings by a Cuban artist named Pablo Cano. In one, Adam and Eve look perfectly happy standing under a tree that holds a smiling snake with little ears. In the other, Adam and Eve look terrified as a fierce angel with a flaming sword chases them out of the garden. The drawings remind me of how it all started, and how vulnerable we are. (I don't think Adam and Eve ever had a chance.)

I read a few commentaries to get me going, thinking first about the text, then about the world God loves, and finally about the particular congregation I will address. Since I am always a guest preacher now, I also imagine myself in the particular space, which I research as carefully as I can. Will it be a modern space or a traditional one? Are the windows made out of stained glass or clear? Is the pulpit high or low? What are the preaching customs in that place? What kind of sermons are people used to hearing? Do people sit close to the front or far away? Will my voice be amplified, and if so, where are the speakers in relationship to the pulpit? I find out everything I can.

Even if I don't know everything about the congregation, I think I know the basics. I know that they wake up in the middle of the night and worry about things they cannot do anything about. I know that they want more love, or want to love more, and that they have longings inside them that they cannot name. I know that they wonder about God and whether other people hear or see more God than they hear or see. I know that they wonder what will happen to them when they die.

When I was in a big-city church, I counted on a weekly Bible study with parishioners to help me prepare to preach. When I moved to the country, that proved less helpful, because the people who came were pretty protective of the text and seemed more afraid to ask questions. So I gathered a smaller, more informal circle of people whom I would regularly consult about a sermon—a friend who was raised a Christian but who now practices Sufism, a nineteen-year-old college student, a clergy colleague whose sermons I love, and—most importantly—my patient husband, who is my number one theological discussion partner and trusted sermon critic. When I was in full-time parish ministry, my relationship with the musician was also very important. Since he had a Masters of Divinity as well as a Ph.D. in music, he was a valuable liturgist. Together we planned weekly worship as well as special liturgies, at which he was often the officiant.

My preaching collaborators also include *The New York Times,* National Public Radio, *Vanity Fair, The Christian Century, Tricycle* (a Buddhist journal), and *Parabola*—all of which take me beyond my immediate context and remind me of the larger world in which my listeners and I live. I rely heavily on the work of biblical scholars as well. They are part of my preaching community, and I honor them as colleagues who have devoted more time to studying the text than I will ever do. I count on them to curb my sometimes wild imagination and to remind me where the boundaries are.

I try to stay away from weekly preaching sheets, because I am vain enough not to want to sound like everyone else who used that particular preaching sheet this week. I tend to reach for more primary texts—biblical commentaries, pertinent theological works, or topical volumes that relate to the sermon. I am slowly building my library of commentaries by Jewish authors. When I work on passages from the Hebrew Bible, I try to make sure that I honor the Hebrew understanding of the text. I think that Christians often do terrible violence to Hebrew texts, characterizing Jews and Jewish thinking in ways that most Jews would not recognize.

I write on lined paper with a pencil, using my computer strictly as a word processor. I like using the pencil because I can produce *eraser dust.* If I ever doubt my efforts, I can always look at the eraser dust and be assured that I really have been working very hard.

In the first half of the process, I give a good deal of time to "checking the nest." During this phase, I go about my business and let the sermon ideas incubate, coming back periodically to see if an egg has appeared. I hang the laundry out on the line, feed the horses, pick peas for supper. The point is to pay divine attention to the world and all the creatures who are in it. If I am eating badly, sleeping poorly, neglecting my friends or my exercise routine, then I know that my preaching is going to suffer. My house is my giant metaphor for what kind of shape my life is in. When the dust balls reach two inches in diameter and everything in the refrigerator smells bad, then I know it is time to slow down and revisit my priorities.

Other helpful preaching practices include watching movies, reading poetry, rearranging the hay in the hayloft, taking long walks, and getting out of the country at least once a year.

Structuring the Sermon

The hardest part of sermon preparation comes after the egg shows up. I try to rewind my process so that I start back where the congregation will start when they hear the passage in church. By now, I have put in ten or twelve hours on it and am way ahead of them. So how am I going to back up? I begin by reading the passage aloud and imagining how it might reverberate in the bodies of these particular people. What emotions might they be feeling right after they have heard that? What images are strong? What might sound offensive to them, or comic, or strange? Then I try to begin there, where they might be likely to begin.

Next, I do something that I think I stole from Fred Craddock. I think about the sermon in terms of orientation, disorientation, and reorientation. I actually write the letters one under the other on a page—*O, D, R*—and try to fill in the blanks. Orientation has to do with what we all know, or think we know, about this text. That is my first goal: to start with some shared perspective on the passage at hand. That will give people a chance to settle down with me as I try to establish my trustworthiness with them.

If I can do that, then chances are better that they will stay with me when I introduce a little bit of disorientation into the conversation.

The disorienting point, for me, is whatever shifts my perspective on the text. It often corresponds to the spot where I became most interested in my own study of it. For instance, I just read the Adam and Eve passage again and realized, for the first time, that the snake told the truth and God lied. Well, that's very interesting and also a little disturbing. I am not sure where I would go with that in a sermon, but that is the kind of thing I am looking for at this second stage of the game. What upsets the balance?

But I don't want to leave people disoriented, so the third stage is reorientation. Once the passage has been tipped off balance, how does it settle down again? What I hope for here is some shift in perspective—even if it's only five degrees—so that the passage gains a new hearing. None of this is manufactured for the congregation, by the way. If I don't experience a shift in the way I see things, then neither will they. If there is no sense of discovery for me, then there won't be one for them either. So it is important that I hold out for some kind of revelation and then report it as best I can.

While I officially believe that preachers should experiment with all kinds of sermonic structures, this one is my old reliable. Gene Lowry likes it, too, and speaks of it in terms of "plotting the sermon." At the very least, it keeps me from delivering sermons in which I tell you something I already know that I think you should know too. In my preaching life, the gospel simply does not lend itself to that kind of certainty. Good news remains divinely disorienting for me.

On the Use of Personal Stories

The reason personal stories are dangerous and the reason I use them are the same: the voyeurism involved. People may become more interested in what I am up to than in what the text is up to, and that is where it goes awry. But what they are listening for, I think, is some evidence that they are not as crazy as they think. That is why they watch and listen to other people—to decide how normal or abnormal they really are. At least, that is what makes me a voyeur. So by using personal stories in sermons, what I mean to be doing is offering my listeners a little chunk of our common humanity, so that they can say, "Oh, you too? What a relief!"

My rule is to refrain from using "I" material unless I think that my listeners can say "me too." I don't always succeed, but that is the goal. I try to act as a roving reporter more than as the star of my own show. The point is for people to see themselves, not me, but sometimes it is safer for them to do that sideways, by identifying with me. More and more, I let my husband Ed be the hero in my stories. He is the faithful, loving servant, and I am the rigid, obsessive-compulsive person who just does not get it. But even in that case, I have to exhibit some kind of compassion toward myself—especially if I want my counterparts in the congregation to "get" God's compassion toward them.

I am persuaded that creativity takes place in the perceptual phase of thinking, which means that telling good stories depends on cultivating good observation skills. It is important to hear the difference between how a cardinal sounds and how a bluebird sounds. It is important to be able to tell the difference between a daffodil and a jonquil. Why? Because it means that you are paying attention. Because it is a sign to God that you are ready to pay attention to other things that may be more difficult to discern. If I am attentive enough to life in this world—if I learn to see well enough—then occasionally God allows me to see through to another kind of life in another kind of world. But I cannot skip over this world. The only way there is to be here now.

On Writer's Block and Anxiety

I have only had two attacks of writer's block—both times when I had placed myself under terrible pressure to produce a work of art. If we can let ourselves off that hook, then there is almost always something faithful and fairly intelligent that we can say about a specific text to a specific people at a specific time in their lives. The two times I have gotten blocked, I just did the best I could and then abandoned the sermon so that I could get a couple of hours' sleep before I had to go to church. Both times, I don't think anyone but me noticed how bad it really was.

My crisis usually comes *after* I have written a sermon. After I have built it from scratch with my own hands, after I have taken it apart three times, put it back together again, and polished every phrase, there generally comes a moment right before the service starts when I look at it and think, "That is so obvious. That is so dumb. Everybody knows that already, and you are about to put them all asleep." I panic at the end of the process, but once the opening hymn starts, I usually recover. After the praying starts, the anxiety goes away. I remember that this is a worship service, not a solo performance, and that God promised to show up.

The Heart of My Preaching

I aim to be a biblical preacher. I begin with what I believe the text meant in its original context. Then I develop that meaning as imaginatively as I am able, until it begins to sound like a meaning that might be illuminative now. I try to use simple language and images. My goal is always to describe both the text and the world in ways that sound truthful to my listeners and to persuade them of the divinity that is present in every moment of their lives.

I am more aware of my limitations as I age and travel. Wherever I preach, the bulletin should carry a disclaimer that says, "Please remember that the preacher is a white, upper-class American woman who has never even broken a bone." The gospel I preach has a lot to do with the goodness of incarnation, but more and more I am aware that I can preach that because I don't live in a Sudanese refugee camp. I'm not trying to hide my kids from the guys with machetes or figuring out how to feed them on air. I preach from a position of cultural privilege, which makes my own words sound more and more hollow to me. My only consolation prize is that I preach to people in positions of cultural privilege, so perhaps I know them well enough to say something to them that they can hear—not to blame them, or to make them feel guilty, but to invite them into a wider world than the one both they and I live in.

More and more, it seems to me that the gospel is terrible news before it is good news—especially if you happen to be at the front of the line, on the top of the heap. That seems to be where I am being led these days—to the gospel that disturbs before it comforts and that insists on death as the condition of new life.

Preparing for Delivery

I am more interested in the physical act of preaching now than ever before. I listen to more sermons than I preach these days, which has given me the opportunity to pay attention to everything that is going on behind, above, and through the actual words that are spoken. I am interested in the way preachers move, in the way they use their hands. I am interested in how they look at people—or don't—and what their voices tell me about their comfort inside their own bodies. It is not "good" voices or "bad" voices that I am listening for, but voices that come from somewhere near the heart and that do not seem afraid to be heard. Or if they are afraid, then they are still willing to be heard, and that courage makes them worth listening to.

While we are preaching, I don't think that many of us can bear to think about how revealed we are. We think we are hiding behind our scholarship, our narrative skill, our repartee, but the truth is that we are just hanging out there, stark naked in front of all those people. According to the experts, about 93 percent of what people get from us is not the words we have so carefully chosen but our own embodiment of the word—the way our voices and bodies do or do not match up with our messages of love and grace and forgiveness.

Different preachers make different decisions about that unavoidable self-revelation. I have women friends who wear the most fantastic earrings they can find when they preach. They wear red lipstick and make sure the collars of their dresses show over their vestments. The message is, "Look, I am a woman: Deal with it." I tend to go in the opposite direction, perhaps because I was never all that successful at "girl things" growing up. I didn't want Barbie dolls. I wanted my daddy to teach me how to shoot a gun. Whatever the deep-seated reasons are, I try to look as vanilla as I can. I wear the tiniest possible earrings, the blackest flats, as little make-up as possible. But when I go to get a haircut, I ask for something slightly—*je ne sais quoi*—free-spirited. I don't want a helmet haircut. I don't want to look totally pulled together. The point, I suppose, is that we all have choices, and the best thing we can do is to be aware of them.

When I was in full-time parish ministry, everything I wore was black or gray or black-and-gray. Now that I am teaching, I wear a lot of blues and greens—even red on occasion! I love having colors back in my life, although I am aware that no one but me ever said that I could not have them. In the parish, I just felt this tremendous responsibility to be a neutral shepherd. I did not want to exercise my individuality in any way that would be a stumbling block for anyone. It was hard enough for some of them to have a woman rector, without my pressing the point.

As for the actual words on the page, I do use a full manuscript, although I mean to use it as a kind of play script or musical score. I feel sorry for manuscript preachers. So many of us feel inadequate. We have bought the idea that preachers who are *really* empowered by the Holy Spirit don't need to write anything down on paper. They just open their mouths when the time comes and gold coins fall out. I am susceptible to that fantasy, but I try not to let it deflate me. Using a manuscript is not the point. The point is *how I use* a manuscript.

I compose for the ear, not the eye. That means that I use the simplest language and syntax that I can. I make it sound conversational on purpose, and I try to introduce new images or ideas slowly enough to let them develop in the ear. In a way, my writing is more like transcribing an oral monologue.

By the time I deliver a sermon, it is almost entirely inside of me. The manuscript is there like a musical score, to make sure I don't forget the movement or the tempo, but my goal is not to look at it while I am talking. The few times I have departed from my "score" have been pretty disastrous. The problem is that I free-associate very easily and end up saying a lot more than I meant to say. Pretty soon I am ten miles away from where I meant to be and have to scramble to get back. Either that or I tell stories using language that really does not belong in church.

I did prepare for an entirely oral presentation once. I had prepared to preach at a formal eleven o'clock service, but when I arrived I discovered that I was supposed to preach at an informal nine o'clock service as well. The smaller space and the seating-in-the-round both made a manuscript seem out of the question. So I went into a back room, reduced the sermon to its essence, and tried out a couple of different ways of saying it while I paced back and forth. When I thought I had the ideas and images in line, I went out and participated in the worship service (which was more like an AA meeting and very wonderful). When the time for the sermon came, I just stood up, connected with my listeners, and gave a very short homily. It was exhilarating—like rappelling for the first time—and I knew that I could learn to do that more often if I took the time. So far, I have not taken the time.

Neither do I spend much time rehearsing out loud. I may read a sermon out loud to find out where my tongue won't go, but I don't do a full dress rehearsal. The reason is that I want to experience the sermon fully for the first time along with my listeners. I want to save every bit of my energy—and my potential for being surprised—for that occasion.

The congregation plays a huge role in my preaching, both as I am writing and as I am speaking. They are on my mind from the moment I sit down to compose a sermon. As I write, I imagine their objections and their questions as well as their emotional state. I think of everything I have ever heard from them about what makes a sermon wretched or wonderful, and I try to take their advice. I choose my language with them in mind, and I reach for images that I believe will make sense to them.

Then, when we are finally all in the same room together, I start this silent, earnest effort to connect with them. It is really quite mystical, which makes it impossible to talk about. The point is that I surrender myself to the occasion. I will myself to be fully present from the top of my head to the soles of my feet. I crank open the doors of my heart and ask the Holy Spirit to do something useful with me. And very often I feel the congregation's energy answering mine. I feel what I imagine to be God's energy enriching the whole mix.

This is one of the reasons why I don't believe that anyone can really read a sermon, listen to a sermon on tape, or watch a sermon on a television screen. Every time I hear about someone winning a sermon contest on the basis of a manuscript, I want to protest. That may be a reasonable facsimile of a sermon, but it isn't a sermon, because a sermon is more than words. A sermon is something that happens between people who have consented to spend (at least) a morning of their lives together, listening to one another's stomachs growl, and breathing the same air. A sermon is something that happens in the context of worshiping God. You really do have to be there.

Sermons Require Something of Us

Although I have never set up a post-sermon response group, I believe that it is a very good idea. I am often concerned that preachers have no professional standards that we are required to meet, nor anyone who comes around to see how we are doing. We could probably use some policing, just like people in other helping professions. Can you imagine? There you are, preaching something you pulled together on your way to church this morning, when someone in a dark blue uniform walks down the aisle and says, "I'm sorry, but we can't let you get away with that. You're under arrest." Then she snaps the cuffs on you and leads you away, while your congregation watches with their mouths hanging open.

It is just an idea. But why is it so funny? Are sexual and financial improprieties the only things that can cause preachers to lose their jobs? How about neglecting study and prayer? How about preaching as if nothing were at stake?

Composing a sermon has always been a challenge for me. It has almost never come easily, and if it did, I guess I would be disappointed. I want a sermon to require something of me, the same way I want it to require something of my listeners. I really only have one process, which has remained fairly constant over the years. After twenty years, I may spend an hour or two less than I used to, but I still come pretty close to the old advice about spending one hour in the study for every one minute in the pulpit. This is not simply sermon preparation time, for me, however. It is also Bible study time, theology time, and devotional time. For my congregation, it is pastoral care time, teaching time, spiritual direction time, mission time.

Preachers are always protesting that they don't have the time they need to preach the kind of sermons they want to preach. I know, I know. Life is short, and ordained ministry will always require all the time there is. But if we don't have time to proclaim the gospel, then what *do* we have time for? We have as much time as anybody does. We have all the time there is. All that remains to be seen is what we will do with it.

Bothering God [1]

LUKE 18:1–8

At first reading, Jesus' story about the persistent widow and the unjust judge is one of the funniest in the Christian canon. The humor dissipates, however, with his suggestion that it is a story about prayer. Apparently we too are supposed to make pests of ourselves, in hopes God will respond to us if only to shut us up.

In Luke's gospel the parable follows right on the heels of Jesus' very scary story about the end of the age. "I tell you," he says to his disciples, "on that night there will be two in one bed; one will be taken and the other left. There will be two women grinding meal together; one will be taken and the other left." Then his disciples ask him, "Where, Lord?" And he says to them, "Where the corpse is, there the vultures will gather" (Luke 17:34–37).

Then he takes a breath and continues with the parable of the unjust judge, which is our clue that he is not talking about just any old kind of prayer. He is talking about prayer that asks God to come and come soon—prayer that is more than a little spooked by the idea of being snatched out of bed in the middle of the night—prayer that begs for God's presence, God's justice, God's compassion—not later but right now.

As some of you know, prayer like that can wear your heart right out, if you're not careful—especially when there is no sign on earth that God has heard, much less answered, your prayer. You can only knock so long at a closed door before your hands hurt too much to go on. You can only listen to yourself speak into the silence so long before you start to wonder if anyone was ever there. When that happens—when the pain and the doubt gang up on you to the point that you start feeling dead inside—then it is time to get some help, because you are "losing heart." That is the phrase Jesus uses, and he does not want it happening to anyone he loves. That is why he told his disciples a parable about their need to pray always and not to lose heart.

164

I have a seven-year-old granddaughter by marriage named Madeline. She is blond, skinny, and tall for her age. When she comes to visit, we cook together. Our most successful dishes to date have been mashed sweet potatoes with lots of butter and crescent dinner rolls made from scratch. From the day Madeline was born, we have been able to look each other straight in the eye with no sentimentality whatsoever. The tartness of our love for one another continues to surprise me. It is easy to forget she is seven years old.

When she came to celebrate her birthday last summer, there were just four of us at the table: Madeline, her mother, her grandfather, and I. She watched the candles on her cake burn down while we sang her the birthday song, and then she leaned over to blow them out without making a wish.

"Aren't you going to make a wish?" her mother asked.

"You have to make a wish," her grandfather said. Madeline looked as if someone had just run over her cat.

"I don't know why I keep doing this," she said to no one in particular.

"Doing what?" I asked.

"This wishing thing," she said, looking at the empty chair at the table. "Last year I wished my best friend wouldn't move away but she did. This year I want to wish that my mommy and daddy will get back together…"

"That's not going to happen," her mother said, "so don't waste your wish on that."

"I know it's not going to happen," Madeline said, "so why do I keep doing this?"

Since the issue was wishing, not praying, I left her alone that afternoon, but I know that sooner or later Madeline and I are going to have to talk about prayer. I do not want that child to lose heart. I want her to believe in a God who loves her and listens to her, but in that case I am going to have some explanation ready for why it does not always seem that way.

This is the same problem Jesus was having with his loved ones. Things were not going well in the prayer department. The disciples wanted God to make clear to everyone that Jesus was who they thought he was, but instead there were warrants out for his arrest, and even he was telling them that his place at the table would soon be empty. By the time Luke wrote it all down twenty years later, things had gotten even worse. Rome was standing over Jerusalem like a vulture over a corpse, and there was no sign of the kingdom coming any time soon. Jesus had said he would be right back, only he was not back. People were losing heart, so Luke repeated the story that Jesus had told about the wronged widow who would not stop pleading her case.

Luke does not say what her complaint is about, but it is not hard to guess. Because she is a widow, her case probably concerns her dead husband's estate. Under Jewish law she cannot inherit it—it goes straight to her sons or her brothers-in-law—but she is allowed to live off of it, unless someone is trying to cheat her out of it. The fact that she is standing alone in the street is a pretty good indicator that none of the men in her family is on her side. If she had any protectors left, they would have kept her home and gone about things in a more civilized manner. No son wants his mother hanging the family laundry in the street. No brother-in-law wants his brother's widow disgracing the family name.

But she has no one holding her back, and as the judge soon finds out, she is quite capable of taking care of herself. This is not a respectable judge, remember. By his own admission, he has no fear of God or respect for anyone. Maybe he thinks that makes him a better judge—more impartial and all that—or maybe he has sat on the bench long enough to know how complicated justice really is. However it happened, he is very well-defended. God does not get to him and people do not get to him, but this widow gets to him, at least partially because she throws a mean right punch.

We cannot hear the humor in the English translation, but in Luke's Greek version, the judge uses a boxing term for the widow. "Though I have no fear of God and no respect for anyone," he says, "yet because this widow keeps bothering me I will grant her justice, so that she may not wear me out with *continued blows under the eye*" (author's translation). His motivation in responding to her is not equity but conceit. He does not want to walk around town with a black eye and have to make up stories about he got it. Anyone who has seen the widow nipping at him like a mad dog will know where he got it. Since he cannot stand that idea, he grants her justice to save face.

"Listen to what the unjust judge says," Jesus says to his disciples. This is the part he wants us to pay attention to. *Won't God do the same for you? If you too cry out both day and night, will God delay long in helping you too?*

I am trying to decide whether I really want to tell Madeline this story. What if she concludes that the way to get what she wants is to keep punching God under the eye? Worse yet, what if she gathers that God will answer her not in order to draw her closer but in order to get rid of her?

Actually, I don't think I will say much about God at all. I think I will focus on the woman instead—about how, when she found herself all alone without anyone to help her, she did not lose heart. She knew what she wanted and she knew who could give it to her. Whether he gave it or not was beyond her control, but that did not matter to her. She was willing to say what she wanted—out loud, day and night, over and over—whether she got it or not, because saying it was how she remembered who she was. It was how she remembered the shape of her heart, and while there may have been plenty of people who were embarrassed by her or felt sorry for her for exposing herself like that, there were days when she wanted to say, "Don't knock it until you have tried it!"

She would never have believed it herself—how exhilarating it was to stop trying to phrase things the right way, to stop going through proper channels and acting grateful for whatever scraps life dropped on her plate. There were no words for the relief she felt when she finally threw off her shame, her caution, her self-control and went straight to the source to say exactly what she wanted. She did not know she could roar until she heard herself do it.

Give me justice! she yelled at the judge. *Do your job! Answer me now or answer me later, but I am coming back every day and every night—forever—until you deal with me.*

So he dealt with her, but I am not even sure that is the point. I keep coming back to that sad little question at the end of the parable: "And yet, when the Son of Man comes, will he find faith on the earth?" It makes you think that Jesus did not know too many persistent widows, or at least not enough of them. He did not know too many people with the faith to stay at anything *forever.* Then as now, most people prayed like they brushed their teeth—once in the morning and once at night, as part of their spiritual hygiene program.

Even the ones who invested more of themselves than that tended to be easily discouraged. They would hang in there for a while, maybe praying as much as an hour a day for weeks on end, but when those prayers seemed to go unanswered, they would back off—a little or a lot—either by deciding not to ask so much or by deciding not to ask at all. Superficial prayers turned out to be less painful than prayers from the heart, and no prayers turned out to be the least hurtful of all. Don't ask, and you won't be disappointed. Don't seek, and you won't miss what you don't find. As for that growing deadness they felt where their hearts used to be, well, they would just have to get used to that.

What the persistent widow knows is that the most important time to pray is when your prayers seem meaningless. If you don't go throw a few punches at the judge, what are you going to do? Take to your bed with a box of Kleenex? Forget about justice altogether? No. Day by day by day, you are going to get up, wash your face, and go ask for what you want. You are going to trust the process, regardless of what comes of it, because the process itself gives you life. The process keeps you engaged with what matters most to you, so you do not lose heart.

One day, when Madeline asks me outright whether prayer really works, I am going to say, "Oh, sweetie, of course it does. It keeps our hearts chasing after God's heart. It's how we bother God, and it's how God bothers us back. There's nothing that works any better than that."

CHAPTER 11

Mary Donovan *Turner*

The faculty at Pacific School of Religion was invited to plan the community's weekly worship service to be held on May 9, 2000. The service is fashioned around the lectionary texts for the following Sunday, in this case the readings for the Fourth Sunday of Easter, Year B. Usually in these services proclamation takes the form of homily or sermon; occasionally communion is served. The Tuesday morning chapel is the singular community-wide worship experience of the week, though smaller groups often meet, practicing varied forms of meditation, liturgical dance, and song. I was named preacher for the May 9 service.

Pacific School of Religion is an interdenominational seminary in Berkeley, California. It is a liberal Protestant seminary on the Pacific rim. Its location in the San Francisco Bay area affords it access to a wide variety of cultures and their unique expressions. PSR has recently invested itself in three initiatives. One is a center for gay and lesbian studies, which is envisioned as a conversation place about sexual orientation and gender—issues that are fraught with emotion and that threaten almost every mainline Protestant group in America. Another initiative seeks to develop leadership for Pacific Asian North American communities. Yet another is exploring conversations between faith and health by bringing medical personnel, community planners, public health experts, and theologians into conversation with one another. Each of these initiatives demands critical thinking and an understanding of contextuality—the varied ways each community comes to know, learn, and experience the world. PSR is one of nine seminaries in the Bay Area that have joined together in a consortium called the Graduate Theological Union. Students who choose to study here do so oftentimes because, in this environment, they can be exposed to diverse cultures, theologies, and traditions. Through the GTU Centers students are able to gain exposure to other world religions (Buddhism, Judaism), which enables them to put their own faith traditions and communities into conversation with others. This conversation is highly valued among us.

As I thought about the community, I was aware that it was only two weeks until graduation and that many, many students were in the throes of great transition. They were thinking about their future ministries with both excitement and dis-ease. They were overwhelmed by fear and unbounded hopes for whatever lay ahead. Middler students were finishing their field education placements both affirmed and aware that they had much to learn in their one remaining year on the PSR campus. Freshman and middler students were writing papers, which prompted them to think about vocational goals, theological questions, and the challenges of ministry. In classes and through these evaluative papers students were trying to reflect on thorny theological issues related to authority (biblical, personal, and communal), theodicy, and ecclesiology. Where would these questionings lead them?

The Texts

A first reading of the lectionary texts reminded me that the Psalm would be the sole selection from the Old Testament, because readings from Acts substitute for the law, prophets, or writings in the Easter season. I was initially disappointed, because virtually all of my preaching is done from Old Testament texts. That is because my educational background is primarily in Old Testament studies. It is also because many Protestant communities have little opportunity to hear preaching from its texts. I read the lections (Acts 4:5–12, Ps. 23, 1 Jn. 3:16–24, Jn. 10:11–18) about three weeks before the assigned chapel date. An early reading of the texts allows me the opportunity to live with them, pray with them, immerse myself in them, see the community's experience through them, and, at the same time, see the texts through the experience of our community and the wider world. Since most of my preaching is now done within communities I do not know, preaching at PSR gave me a welcome opportunity to preach within a community that is familiar and close. At least I know some of its strengths, its challenges, and its moods.

There are several metaphors explicit in the readings for this Sunday of Easter; they are primary and easy to identify. The first, of course, is that of the shepherd. In the gospel reading I was taken by the notion of the "good" shepherd, thinking that "good" in the seminary community has come to define work that is not exceptional, that is only acceptable, perhaps average. The images of the life-giving one, the dedicated one who is known by his/her voice, held forth promise for proclamation in the seminary environment. This metaphor, of course, is reinforced in Psalm 23. I noted that it would be a challenge to preach from a text so familiar. First John and its emphasis on service in not only word but also speech and action, its implicit imperative to be aware of the needs of those in the world around us, would both reinforce and challenge those who were soon to leave the community and begin varied ministries in a world filled with need. But it was the reading of Acts that caught me, not because it would be affirming of the community and not because it was consistent with many of the theologies held by PSR students. Not because it would be easy! Much of the discussion around chapel services throughout the year had been around interfaith worship—how do we, can we, should we make manifest in our weekly services a sensitivity, acceptance, or affirmation of truth claims made by other religions? How do we hold onto the Christian foundation of the community and its constituents and, at the same time, honor the diversity among us? I read these words from Acts 4: "This Jesus is 'the stone that was rejected by you, the builders; it has become the cornerstone.' There is salvation in no one else, for there is no other name under heaven given among mortals by which we must be saved" (vv. 11–12). Here, I thought, in these words from Peter to the rulers, elders, and scribes, is the greatest challenge for this community of worshipers. Here, and in Peter's staunch claim about the singular authority that undergirds his work, is the tension, the disequilibrium, the dynamic and challenging word from which a sermon could grow.

With these preliminary thoughts I met with the chapel planning team to begin to think about this text in light of worship. We read the text together and identified the words, images, and themes that immediately caught our attention. We were aware that the limits of the text needed to be extended in order to set more clearly the context in which the conversation between the council and Peter took place. Acts 4:5 begins with "The next day..." The next day after what? What do we need to know about the experiences of Peter before the questioning? We were fascinated with the bold speech of the disciples, PSR now trying to begin some bold initiatives of its own. These initiatives will endeavor to give public voice to our own understandings of pervasive oppressive systems and a gospel that speaks of inclusivity, which calls us to acknowledge and locate ourselves in those places where the sharp divisions among us promote fear and mistrust. We were impressed by the assertive speech and the acknowledgment in the story that there are pervasive forces in the world and in ourselves that seek to silence truths.

The Pattern

My process begins with my own encounter with the text, not someone else's. Work with commentaries must come later. I do a "close read" of the assigned lections. Sometimes I "learn" the text, because this forces me to pay attention to every word and detail that might be missed in a more casual read. This close read brings to the forefront repeated words or themes that need to be recognized. Work with Greek and Hebrew concordances often provide vital information about the nuances of the text's vocabulary that could lend important theological or literary insight.

A close read of Acts 4 confirmed that "bold" is an important theme in this story of Peter and John and their imprisonment. Verses 13, 29, and 31 attest in this way to the powerful witness of the disciples. A vast assortment of words related to speech, voice, and word underscore that the story is about verbal, public, persistent proclamation. What memories does this story provoke? What emotions? What thoughts? What questions? What myths or misperceptions does it challenge? Where does it confront us? comfort us? Who were the various characters in the story? What was the experience of each? What do I see, hear, feel, taste, smell? Is there anything in this story that makes me afraid? calls me to confession? instills a deep sense of gratitude, wonder, awe? What challenges does this text pose? What surprises? I began to write down my responses to these questions over the next week that followed. Since I have worked for several years on understanding the "voice" in relation to preaching, metaphorically and physically, a whole range of historical narratives came to my consciousness, stories about women and men who had, in the face of oppression, found boldness. I thought about my own struggle to become a "voiced" person, and though these first-person narratives did not become a part of the sermon, their remembering did provide the sense of urgency and importance out of which the sermon and its delivery grew. I put myself in front of the council, wondering what my own response to their questions would be. Would they be like Peter's? not like Peter's? I mentally put myself in the classroom with the beginning preaching students at PSR and became aware of the deep and constant longing I have that they begin to find and strengthen their own voices. I knew that I wanted them to be able to speak about authority without flinching and be able to name and articulate their own. By what authority do they preach? minister? silence another? Are we to feign that this is a gospel without power?

A conversation with a colleague about this text (sermon writing need not be a solitary endeavor!) reinforced the discomfort our shared community would have with its hearing. Who among our community talks openly about the resurrection? What is our response to evangelistic zeal and fervor? We do not want to offend, and there is a hesitancy, a theological one, to claim a certainty about what we know. PSR has set as its goal, and invites all who come, to be challenged by looking at the world and at religious texts, especially sacred texts, through diverse cultural experiences and through the eyes of those who have been left out. PSR invites us to engage critically the world and its diversity as maturing and discerning leaders. How do we speak with boldness about our own experiences, recognizing that varied contexts might and will provide experiences radically different from our own? This text poses a strong challenge to liberal Protestants who find it much easier to boast that what we do, whatever we do, is by our own might, intellect, bodily strength, technical power, or sheer hard work. It is much easier to say that than to name God's power at work in us.

I do a great deal of study about the texts from which I preach. To learn everything I can about a text, whether or not that information is made explicit in the sermon, provides a confidence and a foundation for interpretation that often subtly, but importantly, does its work. I read a wide variety of commentaries, from those that focus on lexical and text critical observations to those that begin to make an interpretive leap for the preacher and may even be lectionary based. I have learned that it is important to read commentaries with a "hermeneutic of suspicion" in the same way we read a biblical text. And it is important to read commentary material written by women and by those who live in radically different contexts so that we can get a full-orbed sense of the many truths and insights the text has to offer. Work with commentaries is important even if there is only a single word or phrase that is helpful; still, even these can completely alter the sermon's development. A look at the commentaries can provide a new question, lend a new perspective, or correct a misguided interpretation or insight.

Commentaries dedicated to discussion of Luke-Acts remind us that the literary context for this story is the whole of the Luke-Acts narrative. It is important to see the experience of Peter in light of the passion narratives at the end of the gospel and the experience at Pentecost at the beginning of Acts. What recent experiences would have shaped Peter's understandings and fueled his boldness? How did he as an "ordinary man" find both words and courage to articulate his own answer to this question: "By what power or by what name did you do this?" (Acts 4:7). A singular read of Acts provides the answer to that question. When the Holy Spirit makes an appearance in this narrative about the early church, an individual or a community is brought to speech. In this story, it is God working through God's Spirit in the world that makes bold and courageous speech possible.

There is some ambiguity in this story about Peter and John's being brought before the council of the rulers, elders, and scribes assembled in Jerusalem. It is not clear if the concern of the people is that Peter and John and others have been proclaiming the resurrection of the dead or if the problem is that the lame man at the Beautiful Gate of the temple was, the day before, healed by Peter in the name of Jesus Christ of Nazareth. Either way, the issue is that of authority. And it is here that I decided the sermon should or could have its focus. We had recently wrestled with the word *authority* in a basic preaching class. When I asked the students to call out what the word meant to them, the responses were varied: power, control, manipulation, rule, judge, command, foundation, rootage, leadership, and others. It was clear that the class was divided about the meaning of authority and whether or not they wanted any. As in Acts 4, I linked speaking with authority and speaking with fervor/boldness. My sermon for the PSR community was an invitation to name their authority(ies) and speak. With this focus now in place, I was able to make decisions about material that should or should not be included. Deciding what valuable information and which wonderful stories do *not* have a rightful place in *this* sermon is an important step in good sermon development.

Perhaps the most pervasive change in my preaching is that, over the years, I have come to trust the expression of my own life experiences. It has been difficult to trust my own experience's relevancy and importance. Sometimes the prophetic task is learning to value others; sometimes it is learning to value self. As the days passed, several personal experiences that I thought were helpful to the sermon came to mind. I have learned to trust that this will happen, that if the preacher does her work, expressions of the fullness of the text will come. The first experience (the first memories and insights are not *always* the best) to come to mind was a story about my then ten-year-old son who unexpectedly one evening taught me something about bold speech. Listening to the radio the week before the sermon was to be preached, I heard an interview with a man who had studied in depth five of the world's most famous singers. He read about them and extensively interviewed them. When the author was asked if there was a message for the listening community that came out of his experience with these five, he said, "Yes, and it is this. Don't die with your music still inside you." Only because I had already started to work on this sermon well in advance did I hear the words spoken so powerfully; I was seeing and hearing the varied and multiple experiences of daily life through the story of Peter and John. From this experience the understanding of voice and emboldened speech took a turn toward metaphors related to music and song. What is it that we in the PSR community want and need to be singing? What is our particular song? With this metaphor now a guiding one, I selected the historical narrative of Anna Julia Cooper out of many that could be shared on this occasion. The witness of the nineteenth-century African American woman enhanced the stories of Peter and John, I thought, because she provided the testimony of a strong woman who found her voice, her song, in the face of the many oppressions the world forced on her.

Although it was not possible in this instance, it is here in the process that I would normally search out artistic expressions of the biblical text. Paintings throughout the centuries provide interesting interpretive insights that may contradict or reinforce our own. It is sometimes the painting that can lead us to understand how context influences our understanding. It may invite us to ask a new question through its own inherent/implicit narrative quality.

At the next chapel planning meeting we talked about voice and the metaphor of song. We decided to begin the service in silence, and then a single voice would sing—"How Can I Keep from Singing?" The service would close, with the faculty leading the community in "Lift Every Voice and Sing." The prayers reminded us to remember the voices in the world crying out in lament, in desperation. Communion would be served, and in anticipation of it I added to the sermon the imagery of those for whom the bread is nonexistent and the cup is always bitter. On behalf of these we want our voices to be strong.

I tried, as I wrote this sermon, to use language that had a "sound" about it that would facilitate getting the sermon heard. I used short sentences. Visual detail. Conversation. Repetition. Questions. I invited the community to take its own place before the council. I put Anna Julia Cooper from the nineteenth century into conversation with Peter. All of this was in an effort to provide the community with an experience of hearing that would, in turn, invite their speaking. The irony of the sermon is that over and over I need reassurance about my own voice. Can the quiet voice of this preacher bear this word? Having made a painful move from silence to voice, the question about my own ability to bring a bold word can plague me. Again, the preacher must preach to the preacher.

Not Silent

ACTS 4:5–12

A few years before moving to the Bay Area, my family and I spent a vacation week in Atlanta, Georgia. Actually, at that time we also lived in Atlanta, Georgia! We were on a tight budget. But we decided to spend the week doing the kinds of things visitors to Atlanta might do. We went to museums and amusement parks. One night we went to watch the Atlanta Braves play baseball. My son Chris at the time was about ten years old, his sister Erin, an infant. We made our way to the stadium, with Chris carrying his baseball glove. His dream was to catch a foul ball hit by a player of either team.

After the fifth inning we were allowed to move to any unoccupied seat in the stadium, and so Chris announced that it was time to look for the perfect place to sit. We got up. Chris led the way. He was followed by Lamar carrying our one-year-old daughter. I was carrying the diaper bag filled with diapers, formula, and handi-wipes. I was also carrying extra jackets, a box of popcorn, two sodas, my purse, the binoculars, and a baby blanket that went with us everywhere. We walked around the perimeter walkway of the stadium to the next section. We walked through the concrete tunnel until we could see the field. "No," Chris said, "This is not right."

So we backed out, walked a little further around the perimeter, into the next section, through the concrete tunnel. Chris looked one way and then the other—"No," he said, "This is not right." We backed out and went to the next section. "Not right." The next. "Yes," he said. "This is it." And so finally we sat down to watch the rest of the game. Next inning. Dale Murphy at bat. Two strikes. Third pitch. Foul ball. Our section. Humanity dives. Dust rises. And out of a tangled mass of arms and legs comes Chris Turner—foul ball in hand! That's the truth.

That night for dinner we ate in a restaurant. After we ordered, Chris got away from the table. We saw him on the other side of the restaurant talking to an older couple, we knew not who they were.

He had the baseball in his hand, and he was going through the motions of describing for them just how it got to be in his possession. When he returned to the table, I said, "Chris, you know, that couple may have come here for a quiet dinner—maybe they wanted to be alone." He said, "Mama, when something is this important, you've got to be telling somebody!"

That's fire in your bones.

That's the men and women of the early church.

It was a customary walk for Peter and John. One they made daily perhaps—to the temple to pray. Three o'clock. Time to go to the temple. Time to pray. But on this day there was a man who had been lame since birth being carried toward the gate. People would often lay him down at the gate of the temple—Beautiful Gate it was called—so that he could ask for money from those who were passing by. He asked Peter; he asked John. But they responded, "Look at us," and when he fixed his attention on them, Peter said, "In the name of Jesus Christ of Nazareth, stand up and walk." And he did.

That's not the end of the story. There's singing and dancing, leaping and thanksgiving, wonder, amazement. There's confusion. For Peter and John, there's prison. There's a hearing. There's anger. There's fear.

Peter and John are brought forth from their cells. Those waiting to hear from them? Rulers, elders, scribes, Annas the high priest, Caiaphas, John, Alexander, and all of the high priestly family—a cast of thousands. By what power or by what name did you do this?

Peter answers, giving witness to his tradition—repeating his own rendition of Psalm 118. Reflecting on his own experience, he said, "In the name of Jesus Christ of Nazareth whom God has raised from the dead. There is salvation in no one else."

Our interfaith sensibilities may be offended here. Because we understand that truth comes packaged in different ways, through different life experiences, we might be offended by this one who seems so sure of one way, his way. Because we like to give every person her God given right to believe as she would like, we perhaps do not like, as Peter, to force our own experiences onto others. And it is much easier for us to boast that whatever we do, it is by our own might, our own intellectual power, bodily strength, or hard work. This is much easier than naming God's power at work in us. We might, for many reasons, be offended by this story.

Emotionally, I must confess, emotionally and physically, I take a step back from Peter. Just as I do when anyone first self-identifies to me as a Christian. It makes me nervous. It makes me very nervous until I know what that means. Because you and I know that there are people in this world who call themselves Christian and who would look me in the eyes and because of what I do here in the place, or look my friends and people I love in the eyes and because of skin color or orientation, would say, "In the name of Jesus Christ…I hate you."

By what authority do we speak another word? What other word is burning inside us? What song do you want to sing? Why is everyone else singing more loudly than we are?

Peter was standing there before the council—did he mean what he said? You bet he did! He had witnessed the empty tomb. The one absolute about life, he had thought, was death. He was in the upper room on the day of Pentecost; the wind swept in and brought with it a power and language—sounds and voices. He witnessed the healing of a man who had been lame since birth. Now—strong legs, strong ankles. This man was standing right there beside him—right on the other side of his skin! A man over the age of forty had had his body restored to health—amazing! (That is the part of the story I can really understand. The amazement that any body over the age of forty could be restored to perfect health!) Peter was giving witness to a life-giving, healing, powerful presence. He knew about fire in the bones; he knew the song he wanted and needed to sing, And he would not be silent.

Anna Julia Cooper. I wish I had known that woman. I have always thought that if I could spend a day in her company, maybe she would be contagious. Maybe something about the way she lived in the world would become my way. But we were separated by place and by time— almost exactly one hundred years between the time she finished her dissertation and I finished mine. She was an African American woman—born in the south, Raleigh, North Carolina. Her mother was a slave, her father her mother's master. In 1892 she published a volume entitled *A Voice from the South*. In it she questioned and challenged the domination of the weak by the strong. She discussed racism, sexism, and classism. She was a victim of all of these.

She tried to discern new metaphors for God—she thought for a while about God as a divine spark, and as a shadow mark, others. But finally she found the metaphor that spoke to her: God as "Singing

Something." This Singing Something within is what, she thought, moves us toward freedom and equality. It is what rises up against domination. God deep within gives rise to a liberating voice. She herself as a black woman was mute and silent. Oppressions (plural) stifled expression, creativity, and fullness. There was, however, something in her. Something that made her tough, resilient. It was vocal. It was auditory. It was God. It was the Singing Something. Thus, she spoke of not being created in the image of God, but in the *sound* of God. God within her—this kind of energy and force that moved her to action—that enabled her to stand next to and up against all the systems that oppressed her.

Peter didn't use the same words as Anna Julia Cooper—but I think he must have known something about that which she spoke. Something about voice. Something about power. Something about speech. Something about oppression. Something about forces, pervasive forces, that seek to silence. Something about boldness. Something about God.

"By what authority did you heal this man?" they asked Peter. And he answered with a boldness they could not explain or understand. When the spirit of God falls down on someone in the book of Acts—they speak. And Peter and John—ordinary people—spoke. And the community asked, "Who are these people? What will we do with them? They will not be silent." So they called them and said, "Do not speak! Do not teach! Do not proclaim!" But they would not, could not keep silent.

What is burning inside you?

I was listening to National Public Radio the other day, and I caught the end of an interview with a man who has just recently finished writing a book about five famous musicians—Pavarotti and others. He had studied their lives, interviewed them, come to know them in ways the world has not. The interviewer asked the author, "What is the message that you want to leave with your readers—can you sum up the one thing you think that these five would want to say to the world?" He said, "Don't die, don't die with your music still inside you."

I have a ritual. I didn't know it was a ritual really—sometimes that's how the most important and meaningful ones grow. So quietly and naturally that you're not even aware of how important they are in your life. This is a graduation day ritual. A PSR graduation day ritual. I make some coffee, and then I read the morning paper. I don't just read it; part of my ritual is that I immerse myself in it. Every year the particularities of the stories change. The names, places, faces— different. But underneath the stories, *the story* is the same. It's about a world that is scarred by division and mistrust and fear. It's about a world in which having is more important than being. Where difference is evil. Where difference may mean death. I read those stories and then I go to graduation and watch women and men walk across the stage, and in my mind I watch them going out into the world, all places in the world. And they begin to speak. And in their ministries they begin to bring communities to speech. They go out to the broken places, the breaches, the divisions, the scarred places— places where bread is nonexistent and the cup is always bitter. They go out to those places and they stay there. And they stay until the people are nourished; the children, women, and men are nourished and they begin to sing. The world begins to hear voices it has never heard before. And soon, and very soon, there is this one large chorus— a song—a bold, passionate, defiant, resistant, and glorious song!

And the world asks, "Who are these people? What are they singing? Why will they not be silent?"

The Preaching Experience

I went over this sermon several times and became familiar with its structure. Because much of the sermon was in narrative form, I knew it would be easy for me to deliver this sermon without benefit of a manuscript before me. I made the following outline, which I took with me to the pulpit so that I could use it to remind me of transitions or words that I did not want to forget.

1. Chris.
2. Story of healing, standing before the council.
3. We may be offended. In the name of Jesus Christ, I hate you.
4. It is as if we are on trial—pulled before the same council.
5. Peter stood in front of them—What was the authority from which he spoke? Did he mean what

he said? You bet he did. Life-giving, healing, powerful presence. He would not be silent.

6. Anna Julia Cooper. Wish I knew her. Dissertation. Metaphors for God. Singing Something within her. Withstanding oppression (s). Liberating voice. Vocal. Auditory. God. Image. Sound.

7. Peter didn't use her words. But he knew something of what she meant.

8. By what authority do you speak? Astounded that this ordinary, uneducated man could speak so boldly. Spirit in Acts. Who are these people? Why won't they be silent? Don't preach. Don't teach. Would not, could not, be silent.

9. Radio.

10. Ritual.

Using the outline provided the security I needed to remember sequence, and at the same time it gave me freedom of movement, eye contact, and vocal expression. I was able to be more focused on the community while at the same time I felt more vulnerable to them. I was able to tell the stories spontaneously. New words and phrasings came to me. New emphases were born in response to the expressions, both facial and verbal, of the listeners. By not using my manuscript, I forfeited some of the wording I had so carefully crafted. But the loss, I thought, was worth it.

When the sermon was over, I felt, as usual, both an exhilaration and a profound sadness that somehow coexist and that I do not yet fully understand. I am affected by the experience in ways I cannot express. It is, I suppose, part of the mystery.

CHAPTER 12

Margaret Moers *Wenig*

I have served as a congregational rabbi, in a single congregation, for sixteen years. The process of sermon preparation has not become easier for me; rather, it has become harder. Because half of my listeners have heard nearly every sermon I have ever given, I cannot repeat myself. Because my congregants are lifelong students, I cannot continue to be their teacher if I stay in the same place theologically or exegetically. As my congregants' understanding of Torah, of God, and of life and death deepens, so must mine. As my sermons improve, my congregants' expectations increase. The bar is constantly raised. To grow every year as a spiritual leader, as a human being, and as a preacher requires a huge amount of time spent in study, prayer, thought, and conversation. Protecting that time is hard for any pastor who is being pulled in many directions. One hour of preparation for each minute of preaching is a necessity. At this stage in my rabbinate, I'd say, it's a minimum.

185

Engaging with the Text

Once, early on in my rabbinate, my congregants took me sorely to task for addressing the text of the weekly Torah reading while ignoring a visit that same week by President Reagan to a military cemetery in Bitburg, Germany. Most of my congregants, at that time, were refugees from Nazi Germany or Jews who fought as American soldiers in WWII. I didn't mention Bitburg in my sermon because I figured I had nothing to add to my congregants' feelings of outrage. I hadn't yet learned that on a week such as that one, more than anything else, my congregants needed their rabbi *to give voice* to what was on their minds. They needed proof from me that I cared about the things they cared about. Until I satisfied that need, they would not listen to anything else I had to say.

This experience taught me that there are always *several* sacred texts present at a worship service. (God speaks to us in many ways.) In our case: the weekly reading from the scroll of the Torah, the corresponding reading from the prophets, the text of the liturgy, the texts of people's lives, the text of the community as a whole, and the text of history. (The Reverend Barbara Lundblad taught me to think of "text" in these ways.) When I am fortunate or doing my job well, I find the intersection of these texts. Sometimes I don't and have to choose among them.

Preaching as Dialogue

I have come to see a sermon as one frame in an ongoing dialogue with my congregation. My best sermons are those that have grown out of conversations with congregants. I try to respond to their explicit or implicit questions, to comments they have made (in classes, in pastoral settings, or in casual conversations), or to reactions that I anticipate they will have to the weekly Torah reading or to current events. Then I try to move the conversation one step forward. If I take my congregants' questions and concerns seriously, then they, in turn, allow me to raise questions or concerns that are on my agenda.

My sermon is never the last word in the dialogue. My congregation has an extraordinary tradition of sitting down and discussing the rabbi's sermon during the coffee hour that follows the service. If there is no coffee hour, congregants walk up to me and tell me their reactions. If for some reason my congregants don't volunteer their reactions, I solicit feedback from several whom I know will be honest with me. I will solicit feedback in particular when a sermon I preached did not elicit the response I had anticipated. Then I try to find out what went wrong. If I can learn from my mistakes, then even a bad sermon or a failed sermon is not a total loss.

If I have been invited to serve as a guest preacher or keynote speaker, I will try talk to several people who are in the host congregation or who are involved in the conference to find out what's on folks' minds. Before a sermon supporting civil marriage for same-sex couples, the keynote speech at a gala conference of gay Jews, I spent many hours on the phone with gay and lesbian opponents of civil marriage. My sermon was largely an attempt to respond to their concerns.

Resources

I have a very poor memory. I compensate by keeping extensive files. I have a file for every weekly Torah reading, every festival Torah reading, and a wide range of topics (euthanasia, handguns, teenagers, sweatshops, work, rest…). When I read something that seems relevant (a newspaper article, poem, passage from a novel), or when I have an idea, I pop it into the appropriate file. My sermon preparation always involves study: reading commentaries on the biblical text (from medieval to modern, though rarely historical/critical) and relevant chapters from books. I write either in my home study, surrounded by an extensive collection of books, or in a library.

Sermons in Series

I have found that there are subjects that cannot be responsibly treated in one fifteen-minute sermon. For the past three years I have devoted all four of my sermons for the Days of Awe—Rosh Hashanah and Yom Kippur—to a single topic. (In 1997, in honor of the one hundredth anniversary of the first Zionist Congress and the upcoming fiftieth anniversary of the founding of the State of Israel, my topic was Zionism. I spoke, in particular, about fashioning a liberal religious Zionism. In 1998, after a year of tragic deaths in the congregation, I devoted all four of my sermons to a discussion of life after death. In 1999, I devoted my sermons to a search for purpose in life.) Giving four sermons in ten days on a single subject allows me to ask questions that cannot be easily answered. It allows time for the entire congregation to become engaged in the conversation with me and with each other. It gives me time to study in depth and give sustained thought to burning issues that I have known little or have thought little about. The series always "ends" on Yom Kippur afternoon, with sermons by four members of the congregation whom I have invited two months earlier and whose perspectives I know will be very different from my own. In fact, the conversation never "ends" then. It usually continues, in private conversations, or now, by exchange of e-mail among many members, for weeks after the final sermon is preached.

Generating Ideas vs. Shaping and Then Editing the Sermon

Dr. Jane Weiss, a writing teacher in my congregation, introduced me to the work of Peter Elbow (*Writing With Power, Writing Without Teachers*). He insists that most writers need to separate the process of generating ideas from the process of shaping and editing. Following his instruction, I include "free writing" as part of my preparation process, after I have read the weekly Torah reading, sometimes after but often before I have studied commentaries on the text. Free writing requires you to write without stopping for a pre-designated period of time (fifteen minutes, a half hour...). You may not lift pen from paper, or fingers from keyboard. You may say anything you wish. If you run out of ideas, you write gibberish, but do not stop writing. This method opens the tap and allows ideas to flow.

Research/study comes next (or if I am feeling particularly dry, it comes first). In preparing "God Is a Woman and She Is Growing Older," for example, I read through the entire one thousand–page orthodox High Holiday prayer book, jotting down all the images of God I liked.

I type my research notes and my own thoughts into the computer one idea to a page as if the pages were note cards. I don't worry about the order of things at this point. Then I print out on scrap paper all that I have typed. I usually have fifty incomplete pages of notes. I may not yet know exactly what I want to say or accomplish through the sermon.

Then I clear a huge space on the floor of my study and begin stacking the pages of my notes into piles. I ask myself, "What pages belong *together?*" I fan out each pile so that I can see each page in it, then I move the piles around until the order seems right. This is the point at which I decide what form I want the sermon to take. Do I want the denouement to be toward the beginning, in the middle, or at the end? When the shape is clear, I remove the pages that no longer fit and see what's missing. What links in the unfolding of the sermon are not yet spelled out? What is still too abstract and requires an accompanying image or illustration? What image or illustration is too subtle and requires an explanation? I return to the computer to fill in the lacunae and compose the connective tissue: beginnings, endings, and transitions.

Then I begin to edit or fine-tune the language of the sermon. Reading the draft aloud helps me find and eliminate awkward spots. This is the point at which I am most likely to ask a colleague or a congregant to listen to my draft; then I will revise it based on their reactions. Needless to say, this is a time-consuming process.

My narrative sermons take shape in a very different fashion. I sometimes use Eugene Lowry's method outlined in *Homiletical Plot* (i.e., "oops!, ugh, aha! whee, yeah").[1] The narrative sermon/midrash I have included in this book follows Miriam's life chronologically. Thus, the order was given.

Propositions

At some point in the process of sermon preparation I articulate (if only to myself) the goal of my sermon. Sometimes I know the goal before I begin preparing the sermon (e.g., to encourage the congregation to reopen our religious school). Other times the goal does not become clear to me until my pages of notes are laid out on the floor. I rarely spell out the proposition in the sermon itself. But I have to know what it is. I learned, from the Reverend James Forbes, to express a proposition in the following form: "I propose to show that _____ to the end that _____" (e.g., to the end that my congregants will think/feel/do *x*). To test the worthiness of the proposition, he taught us to ask: Is the proposition clear? Does the proposition excite your interest? After hearing the proposition, do you want to hear the sermon? Is the proposition urgent? What difference will hearing this sermon make? Is the proposition true to the text? Does the proposition ring true or sound hollow? Does the proposition avoid false advertising, or does it make a promise on which I can't deliver?

Imitation

A course at Auburn Seminary called "Learning to Preach Is Like Learning to Sing the Blues" gave me words for what I had already sensed: that preaching, like a folk art, can be learned by imitating those who are masters. I read and listen to a lot of sermons. I try to analyze each sermon that has affected me. Then I try to imitate techniques the preacher of that sermon used. I don't have time to do this every week, of course. But this method has, over the years, helped me expand my repertoire so that my congregants don't have to listen to the same "type" of sermon week after week, year after year.

Collaboration

When I have time and when I am preaching a sermon for a special occasion, I solicit feedback to *drafts* of my sermons from colleagues or from congregants. I asked two members of my congregation to listen to a draft of the sermon I have included in this book. For eight years I went on retreat with four colleagues two months before Rosh Hashanah. We would brainstorm ideas for High Holiday sermons. As Rosh Hashanah approached, we would read drafts to each other over the phone. When that group ceased meeting, I found three other colleagues with whom to prepare for the Days of Awe. Sometimes we even decided to work on the same topics and shared material or, in the case of three sermons, wrote them collaboratively. Three women, a rabbinic colleague, an academic colleague, and the social worker whom I use for professional supervision (two of whom are not Jews), all pushed me to revise my sermon "God Is a Woman and She Is Growing Older." The final version owes a lot to their criticism of earlier drafts.

Preaching from a Manuscript

I preach from a manuscript. Not because I believe that manuscript preaching is better than preaching from notes—in fact, I wish I could preach from notes alone—but because I am not able to preach without a manuscript. I am not able to remember everything I want to say unless I write it down. I type the manuscript in twelve-point font, double-spaced, in "phrase-a-line." Phrase-a-line means no more than one phrase per line, breaking the line where you would naturally pause in speech. Short lines are easier to read in a glance, and actually writing the sermon in phrase-a-line helps me keep my sentences short and my language simple enough for oral communication. I do not use solid caps, because a graphic designer explained to me that solid caps are harder to read than small-case letters. I use extra white space to help me see where to pause. I mark the typed manuscript with a colored pen, underlining, or putting boxes around words or phrases I want to emphasize. I put in elision marks to remember which words or phrases to link together. I indicate which sections can be spoken quickly and which require a slower, more deliberate delivery. This sort of manuscript takes up many pages. I usually print it on scrap paper. I have to practice the sermon aloud, preferably a few times, so that my head is not buried in my manuscript when I preach the sermon. After the sermon is preached, someone retypes it in a form that is more conducive to circulation, and I add my endnotes.

Health

I find preaching to be an exhilarating and an exhausting process, physically, emotionally, and spiritually. Every time I prepare a sermon, I feel a huge responsibility on my shoulders. I believe that a great deal is at stake. Torah is a Tree of Life. But it is hard work to be ever-worthy to teach Torah. To preach regularly and effectively, I need to be well-rested, eat nutritious meals, exercise, have love in my life, have friends and professional supervision, take time for study, and make time for refreshment (including weekly Sabbath, annual vacation, religious retreat, study leaves, and sabbaticals). I have to have emotional support and sufficient spiritual reserves to plumb the depths of pain, sadness, confusion, and loss in people's lives, to ask the tough questions of God and of myself and emerge from the abyss still holding fast to the Tree of Life.

The Context of This Sermon

I was invited to serve as a scholar-in-residence at a progressive Reform congregation in Washington, D.C. The topic for the weekend was Jewish feminist theology. Because I'm a preacher and not an academic theologian, and because I was scheduled to speak during

Shabbat evening and Shabbat morning services, I offered to give sermons instead of lectures. The weekly Torah reading was Parshat Bo (Exodus 10:1—13:16). I had two goals in mind when preparing this sermon: (1) I wanted to demonstrate the feminist, exegetical technique of giving prominence and voice to female biblical characters; in this case, to give greater depth to the person of Miriam. And (2) I wanted to attempt to reassure a congregation of middle-aged liberals (among whom I count myself) that our dreams for justice and peace will not die, even if these dreams are not all fulfilled in our lifetimes. (The Clinton administration was preparing to invade Iran at the time I was preparing this sermon.)

Before I could speak about Miriam, however, I had to address the age-old question of the hardening of Pharaoh's heart. No one can listen to this text in Exodus without asking, "Why did God harden Pharaoh's heart?" I could not risk addressing any other subject while ignoring this one, so I tackled this one first.

Before the reading from the Torah scroll, I gave a close exegesis of the twenty verses that speak of the hardening of Pharaoh's heart, identified the three *different* Hebrew verbs used, pointed out that in most cases the verbs were either intransitive (Pharaoh's heart became stubborn) or transitive, with *Pharaoh himself,* rather than God, as the subject of the verb (Pharaoh hardened his heart). This exegesis built up to the notion that Pharaoh's lack of responsiveness to reason, his lack of compassion, ultimately defined him. His intransigence became habitual. His character became his destiny.[2]

Before going to D.C., I read a draft of the sermon to two of my congregants. They insisted that I preface the sermon with an introduction in which I review rabbinic techniques of midrash. In general, I prefer to err on the side of assuming that my listeners know things like this rather than assuming that they don't. I make this choice partly because many of my congregants *are* well versed in Jewish learning, and I do not want to bore them with Judaism 101 in sermon after sermon, and partly because I know that listeners who don't have sufficient background to fully understand a sermon of mine will ask questions about it afterwards. But in this case, the congregants whom I had invited to hear my draft were so insistent that I capitulated and provided the following background information in an introduction to the sermon. I am grateful for their insistence.

Introduction

The following sermon is a midrash. Midrash is usually commentary on the Torah in the form of a story. If you are familiar with rabbinic midrash, you will, I hope, recognize the style. If you are *un*familiar with rabbinic midrash, you need to know a few of the operating principles that the rabbis employed and that I employ as well. First of all, the rabbis grant themselves license to *invent* conversations between biblical characters and even to *invent* characters and insert them into the biblical story. The rabbis imagined, for example, that Isaac did not resist his father's attempt to sacrifice him so that he could show up his older half-brother, Ishmael, who had boasted to him, "When our father circumcised me at the age of 13, I did not resist."[3] The rabbis *imagined* the cause of Sarah's death to be her reaction to a visit from Satan, who informed her that her husband Abraham had sacrificed her son.[4]

Now, there is no evidence, in the text, of Ishmael's boasting to Isaac or of Satan's visit to Sarah, but through these imagined conversations the rabbis endeavor to explain elements of the text that are hard to understand: Why didn't Isaac resist his father's attempt to sacrifice him? Why did Sarah die precisely when she did (at the beginning of the *parasha* immediately following the story of the binding of Isaac)? I, too, will invent conversations in order to try to account for elements of the text that cry out for explanation.

Second, the rabbis take the liberty of weaving together verses and information from a wide variety of sacred sources, often without identifying them. Sometimes a midrash will say, "*k'mo shecatuv:* as it is written," before quoting Torah. But sometimes a midrash just quotes without preface, and the reader either recognizes the quotes, identifies them with the help of a concordance, or relies on a critical edition or annotated translation, complete with footnotes, to provide the biblical sources woven into the midrash. As for their own ideas, sometimes a midrash will credit a given rabbi: for example, "Rabbi Ishmael taught…" but often a midrash speaks anonymously. I, too, will weave together verses and information from sacred sources. Many of you will recognize which words are from the Torah and which words are poetry of Kadia Molodowsky, Adrienne Rich, or Marge Piercy. Or you may consult the footnoted version of the sermon. No part of this midrash is attributed to a R. Ishmael or R. Elazar. It is entirely my own.

Finally, you need to know that it is not unusual in midrash for the rabbis to project back into an ancient story a custom or an institution from their own time. They do this for the sake of filling in an ellipsis in the text. For example, after the story of the binding of Isaac, in which Isaac's life is saved at the last minute, the Torah says, "Abraham returned to the lads and they went to Beersheva and dwelled there." Why does the text say that *Abraham* returned to the lads; why is *Isaac's* name omitted? One answer is found in a midrash that says that Isaac did not accompany his father to Beersheva because Isaac was sent to study Torah with Shem.[5] Well! There was no Torah in Abraham and Isaac's day! But the rabbis insist: "*Ein mukdam v'ein m'uhar batorah.* There is no early or late in Torah." The truths of Torah transcend chronological time. So it is altogether possible in midrash to say that Isaac studied Torah in the Yeshiva of Shem. For what else ought a young man do but study Torah? I, too, will assume the liberty of projecting back into ancient times elements of contemporary culture.

Thus ends my introduction. Following is my sermon. *Yi'yu l'ratson imrei phi vehigyon libi l'fanecha.* May the words of my mouth and the meditations of my heart be acceptable before you.

"Their Lives a Page Plucked from a Holy Book"[6]

Two weeks ago we began reading the opening chapters of the book of Exodus: *"Eleh shemot b'nai Yisrael habaim mitzrayma.* These are the names of the sons of Israel who came to Egypt with Jacob... Reuben, Simeon, Levi, and Judah; Issachar, Zebulun, and Benjamin; Dan and Naphtali, Gad and Asher...Joseph being already in Egypt."[7] So begins a story about seven brave women. *Eleh shemot ha ivriot v'hamitzriot habaot shamayma.* These are the names of the Hebrew and Egyptian women who came close to Heaven: Shifra, Puah, Yochevet, Miriam, Bat Pharaoh, Zipporah, and Elisheva.

There are other brave women in the Torah: Esther, Vashti, Ruth, Naomi... But nowhere else in the Torah do we find so many women mentioned by name or by deed within one story. If you were in synagogue two weeks ago, the characters are fresh in your memory: *Shifra and Puah ham'yaldot,* the midwives, who defy Pharaoh's order to kill all newborn Israelite boys and are rewarded by God with great houses;[8] *Yochevet bat levi,* the mother of Moses, who hides her son until he can be hidden no longer, places him in the river Nile in an ark lined with pitch, and then suckles him as a paid wet nurse;[9] *Miriam achoto,* sister of Moses, who stands watch over her brother and offers to find a wet nurse for him;[10] *Bat Pharaoh,* Pharaoh's daughter, who draws baby Moses out of the water and chooses to raise him;[11] *Zipporah,* Midianite wife of Moses, the mother of his two sons, who saves Moses' life by performing an emergency circumcision;[12] *Elisheva,* daughter of Aminidav, sister of Nachshon, wife of Aaron, who is the mother of Aaron's four sons.[13]

The opening portion of the book of Exodus provides us with a stunning collection of women who resist and defy, women celebrated in feminist haggadot for the roles they played in freeing the Israelites from slavery. So tell me. What happened to these brave women when the men they birthed, nursed, raised, saved, and nurtured were leading the Israelite fight for freedom that resulted in the exodus from slavery and the mass destruction of Egyptian land, livestock, and population? In *Parshat Shemot*,[14] these women risked death to save the lives of their own male babies or to save the lives of sons of their enemies.[15] How could it be that these same women remained silent during the plagues? *Dam, tzefardeya, kinim, arov, dever, shechin, barad, arbeh, hoshech, makat bechorot.*[16]

What were the seven women of *Parshat Shemot* doing during *Parshat Vaerah*[17] and *Parshat Bo*?[18] Where were these women during the plagues? And what became of them after the Israelites left Egypt?

Just as Miriam had stationed herself at a distance to watch her brother Moses in the bull rushes,[19] so too Miriam stationed herself at a safe distance to watch her brothers Moses and Aaron negotiate with Pharaoh. When Pharaoh refused to let the Hebrews go, *"Vayarem b'mateh vayach et hamaim asher bayaor,* [Aaron] lifted up the rod and struck the water in the Nile in the sight of Pharaoh and his courtiers, and all the water in the Nile was turned into blood and the fish in the Nile died. The Nile stank so that the Egyptians could not drink water from the Nile; and there was blood throughout the land of Egypt."[20] "What are you doing?" Miriam asked her brothers when they returned home.

"Pharaoh ordered every male Israelite child thrown into the Nile," Moses answered her, "Now the Egyptians will suffer when the Nile flows with blood. This is God's will." "I don't believe it," replied Miriam, and she left them.

A week later, the negotiations resumed: Once again Pharaoh refused to let the people go; this time Aaron brought a torrent of frogs. Then it was lice. Then swarms of insects. Then a plague that killed Egyptian livestock. Then boils. "Stop this craziness!" Miriam yelled at her brothers. "The Egyptian people want us dead," Moses replied. "Not all of them do," answered Miriam. Miriam sent a message to all the Egyptian women she knew, and they organized a mass letter-writing campaign to convince Pharaoh that the Israelite people were no threat. To no avail. Once again Pharaoh refused to grant Moses' request, and heavy hail and fire rained down, striking all that was in the open: grasses of the field and trees as well.

Intensifying their efforts, a coalition of Egyptian and Israelite women, led by Shifra, Puah, Yochevet, Miriam, Zipporah, Elisheva, and Pharaoh's own daughter, gathered tens of thousands of women in a demonstration of protest against the escalation of the conflict.

Pharaoh was not moved. And a thick mass of locusts ate all of the grass, all of the fruit of the trees not already felled by hail. Egyptians were starving. Insect-borne diseases were rampant, and darkness engulfed the land. But Pharaoh would not let the Israelites go. "*Vayomer Adonai el Moshe v'el Aharon ba'eretz Mitzraim lemor…* The LORD said to Moses and Aaron in the land of Egypt: This month shall mark for you the beginning of months; it shall be the first of the months of the year for you. Speak to the whole community of Israel and say that on the tenth [day] of this month each of them shall take a lamb to a family, a lamb to a household…You shall keep watch over it until the fourteenth day of this month; and all the assembled congregation of the Israelites shall slaughter it at twilight." "*Velakchu min hadam venat'nu al shtei hamezuzot ve'al hamashkotf al habatim…*They shall take some of the blood and put it on the two doorposts and the lintel of the houses in which they are to eat it…For that night I will go through the land of Egypt and strike down every first-born in the land of Egypt, both man and beast…And the blood on the houses where you are staying shall be a sign for you: when I see the blood I will pass over you, so that no plague will destroy you when I strike the land of Egypt."[21]

Miriam spoke to her brother Moses, "How can you go along with this plan? When God threatened to destroy all of Sodom, Abraham argued with him, 'Will You sweep away the innocent along with the guilty?'[22] Surely you will not allow the innocent to die?!" Moses answered her: "Please, if you can obtain our freedom through nonviolent means, this plague will be averted. Be my guest; you have fourteen days." In many regions of Egypt, Israelite and Egyptian women dressed in black, held vigils, marches, sit-ins. Men were among the demonstrators too. Moses and Aaron joined an Israelite hunger strike. But whenever Pharaoh showed signs of softening, his right wing threatened him, and he was forced to hold fast.

Miriam failed to obtain agreement from Pharaoh to release the Israelites. Nothing was left for her to do but to warn the Egyptians and try to protect them: On the thirteenth day, "*Veyishalu ish me'eit rei'eihu ve'isha me'eit re'utah klei kesef uklei zahav.*" As Israelite men and women went from Egyptian house to Egyptian house to ask for objects of silver and gold from their Egyptian neighbors,[23] they warned the Egyptians of the impending danger. And as the Israelites left each

Egyptian home, they put blood on the lintel and the two doorposts of each Egyptian house. *"Vayitein Adonai et cheyn haam b'eyney mitzrayim."* The Egyptians were deeply grateful.[24]

When word reached Pharaoh that the Israelites were seen leaving Egyptian homes with sacks of silver and gold and marking Egyptian doorposts with blood, Pharaoh immediately dispatched his army to arrest the thieves and vandals and to wipe clean the markings of blood from off of the Egyptian doorposts. Yochevet and Elisheva were among those arrested and thrown in prison.[25] The next day, their families left Egypt without them.[26]

Miriam had wanted to be the one to warn Pharaoh's daughter. But she arrived too late. *"Vayehi b'chetzi halaila vAdonai chika kol b'chor b'eretz mitzrayim mebechor Paroah hayoshev al kiso ad bechor hashevi asher beveit habor vechol bechor beheimah.* In the middle of the night the LORD struck down all the first-born in the land of Egypt, from the first-born of Pharaoh who sat on the throne to the first-born of the captive who was in the dungeon..."[27] *"Mi bechor Paroah...*From the first-born of the Pharaoh..." The Torah never mentions a son. Pharaoh's *daughter* was his first-born. (Lest the masculine noun *bchor* lead you to believe that only male first-born were felled, the Haggadah suggests otherwise: *"dam, zefardeya, kinim, arov, dever, shechin, barad, arbeh, hoshech, makat bechorot."* Pharaoh's daughter was among them.)[28]

Miriam failed to arrest the destructive course of the plagues. Moses, on the other hand, finally succeeded in freeing his people. On the far shore of the Reed Sea he sang,

> *"Ah shiral Adonai ki gao ga'ah, sus v'rochvo rama vayam.*
> I will sing to the LORD, for He has triumphed gloriously;
> Horse and driver He has hurled into the sea.
> The LORD is my strength and might;
> He is become my deliverance.
> This is my God and I will enshrine Him;
> The God of my father, and I will exalt Him.
> The LORD, the Warrior—
> LORD is His name!
> Pharaoh's chariots and his army
> He has cast into the sea;
> And the pick of his officers
> Are drowned in the Sea of Reeds."[29]

When the men finished singing their song, "*Vatikach Miriam haneviah et hatof be'yadah.* Miriam the prophetess, Aaron's sister, took a timbrel in her hand, and all the women went out after her in dance with timbrels. And Miriam chanted for them: 'Sing to the LORD, for He has triumphed gloriously; Horse and driver He has hurled into the sea…'"[30] Her voice trailed off. She did not echo the rest of the verses her brother had sung. She was heard only to whisper, "Praise to life, though it crumbled in like a tunnel on ones we knew and loved."[31]

Miriam withdrew from politics after the Exodus from Egypt, emerging only once to challenge Moses' sole authority as a prophet. She was stricken with scales, and Moses himself prayed for her recovery. A midrash in *Sifrei Bamidbar* teaches that Miriam became the wife of Caleb, foremother of Bezalel, or King David. But that's not how I imagine the rest of Miriam's life. I think Miriam spent the remainder of her days as a teacher, a teacher of girls and of her nephews, Nadav and Avihu, Elazar and Ithamar, whose father had ceased to show any emotion[32] after the arrest and disappearance of his wife, Elisheva. Miriam used to tell her nephews stories about their mother, arrested before they were old enough to remember her. "My heart is moved by all I cannot save," sighed Miriam, "so much has been destroyed [and yet] I have to cast my lot with those who age after age, perversely, with no extraordinary power, reconstitute the world."[33] Aaron blamed Miriam for Nadav and Avihu's death.[34] Some days she blamed herself.

No longer did Miriam place herself in the middle of the great conflicts of her time:[35] the battles with Amalek, the building of the golden calf, the report of the spies, the rebellion of Korah. It was the day-to-day work of sustaining a community that drew her in. She used to recite to her students the words of Marge Piercy,

> The people I love the best
> jump into work head first
> without dallying in the shallows
> and swim off with sure strokes almost out of sight.
> They seem to be natives of that element,
> the black sleek heads of seals bouncing like half-submerged balls.
>
> I love people who harness themselves, an ox to a heavy cart,
> who pull like water buffalo, with massive patience,
> who strain in the mud and the muck to move things forward
> who do what has to be done, again and again.

I want to be with people who submerge in the task,
who go into the fields to harvest
and work in a row and pass the bags along,
who stand in the line and haul in their places
who are not parlor generals and field deserters but move in a
common rhythm when the food must come in or the fire be
put out.[36]

Zipporah, the Torah tells us, survived the plagues in safety in Midian, where Moses had sent her and their sons when the trouble started.[37] They saw Moses, once again, briefly, when Jethro brought them to visit at Rephidim. "*Vayetzei Moshe likrat Yitro chotno vayishak-lo.* [Moses] bowed low and kissed [his father-in-law]; each asked after the other's welfare, and they went into the tent."[38] But Moses had no words or embrace for his wife. There was no longer any love between them. Zipporah took the boys back to Midian. They never inherited their father's mantle. They didn't even mourn his death.[39] But Zipporah went on to become a physician, saving lives as she had once saved her husband's life. And her sons after her became doctors in Midian as well. Shifra and Puah did not fare as well. After the death of the firstborn, Shifra went mad and took her own life. Puah died a year later of cancer. Yochevet and Elisheva? No one knows whether they were ever released from prison. Miriam tried to find them after *yetziat mitzrayim*. She never did. "All these lives—like pages torn from a holy book."[40]

> "At night I dream the women of our family come to me and say: We who modestly carried our pure blood through generations, bring it to you like wine kept in the kosher cellars of our hearts."[41]

When Miriam was dying, her mother's words came back to her—words Yochevet once said as her husband was reciting *Eshet chayil.*[42] "Miriam, my mamelah, when they say, 'A woman of valor who can find her worth is far above rubies,' I want you always to remember: A woman's worth is not measured only by what she does in her lifetime. A woman's worth is measured also by what she inspires others to do years, generations after she has died."

A man's worth is not measured only by what he does in his lifetime. A man's worth is measured also by what he inspires others to do years, generations after he has died. So, too, the value of a movement is not measured only by what it accomplishes during its lifetime. The value of a movement is measured also by what it inspires others to accomplish years, generations after the movement has died.

Miriam never married and never had daughters of her own. But among her students, and the students of her students, and the students of her student's students, are numbered: rebels and radicals, legislators and lawyers, poets and painters, teachers and organizers, nurses and doctors, scientists and preachers. And your worth is far above rubies.[43]

NOTES

Introduction

[1]John Calvin, "Sermon XXI sur la Première à Timothée," *Corpus Reformatorum,* ed. Guilielmus Baum, Eduardus Cunitz, and Eduardus Reuss (Brunsvigae: Schwetschke, 1895), vol. 53, col. 376 (author's translation).

Chapter 1: Barbara Shires Blaisdell

[1]Urban Holmes, *Spirituality for Ministry* (New York: Harper and Row, 1982), 156.
[2]Coral Cogbill, private correspondence, September 1998.
[3]John Bunyan, *The Pilgrim's Progress* (Oxford: Oxford University Press, 1984), 23.
[4]Paul Duke, personal correspondence.
[5]Gerald Manley Hopkins, "The Golden Echo," *Poetry and Prose,* ed. Walford Davies (Rutland, Vt.: Charles E. Tuttle, 1998), 73.

Chapter 2: Teresa L. Fry Brown

[1]Elizabeth Barrett Browning, "Sonnets from the Portuguese XLIII," in *Sonnets from the Portuguese and Other Love Poems* (Garden City, N.Y.: Doubleday, 1954), 57.

Chapter 3: Jana Childers

[1]2 Samuel 24:24, author's translation.
[2]For more on this model of creativity, see Paul Scott Wilson, *Imagination of the Heart* (Nashville: Abingdon Press, 1988), 22–27.
[3]Quoted in "The Secrets of Creativity," Anne C. Roark, *The Los Angeles Times,* 12 November 1989, 13.
[4]Anne Lamott, *Bird by Bird* (New York: Pantheon Books, 1994), 6.
[5]Julia Cameron, *The Artist's Way* (New York: G. P. Putnam's Sons, 1992), 9–18.
[6]I was converted to a more collaborative view of preaching by the late Lucy Atkison Rose, whose book *Sharing the Word: Preaching in the Roundtable Church* (Louisville: Westminster John Knox Press, 1997) is but one piece of the important legacy she left the world of preachers. Working with Lucy was one of the great blessings of my life.
[7]Ann and Barry Ulanov, *Primary Speech* (Atlanta: John Knox Press, 1982), 104.
[8]Alfred, Lord Tennyson, "The Higher Pantheism," *The Partial Works of Tennyson,* ed. G. Robert Strange (New York: Houghton Mifflin, 1974), 273.
[9]C. Austin Miles, "In The Garden," in *Melodies of Praise* (Springfield, Mo.: Gospel Publishing House, 1957), 49.
[10]Antoinette Clark Wire, "The God of Jesus in the Gospel Sayings Source," in *Reading from This Place*, vol. 1, ed. Fernando F. Segovia and Mary Ann Tolbert (Minneapolis: Fortress Press, 1995).
[11]I am grateful to New Testament scholar Herman Waetjen for this insight.

Chapter 4: Linda L. Clader

[1]Bruce J. Malina and Richard L. Rohrbaugh, *Social Science Commentary on the Synoptic Gospels* (Minneapolis: Fortress Press, 1992); and idem, *Social Science Commentary on the Gospel of John* (Minneapolis: Fortress Press, 1998).

[2]For the sermon I have included here, my research was much enriched by Raymond E. Brown, *The Birth of the Messiah* (New York: Doubleday, 1993).

[3]For this sermon, I consulted one of my favorite narrative commentaries on Luke, Robert C. Tannehill, *The Narrative Unity of Luke–Acts: A Literary Interpretation,* 2 vols. (Philadelphia: Fortress Press, 1986). He has also written a shorter commentary, *Luke* (Nashville: Abingdon Press, 1996).

[4]Current favorites: *How to Make an American Quilt, Strangers in Good Company, Fried Green Tomatoes*—all of which tell their tales in nonlinear fashion.

[5]Sandra Boynton, *Chocolate: The Consuming Passion* (New York: Workman, 1982), 87.

[6]This homily was preached at the Preaching Excellence Program produced by the Episcopal Preaching Foundation at Catholic University of America, Washington, D.C., May 31, 1999. The sermons and addresses from that conference have been published as *Preaching Through the Year of Luke: Sermons That Work IX,* edited by David J. Schlafer and Roger Alling (Harrisburg, Penn.: Morehouse, 2000). This homily is reprinted by permission of the publisher.

Chapter 5: Yvette Flunder

[1]Henry H. Mitchell and Emil M. Thomas, *Preaching for Black Self-Esteem* (Nashville: Abingdon Press, 1994), 133.

[2]David Buttrick, *A Captive Voice: The Liberation of Preaching* (Louisville: Westminster/ John Knox Press, 1994), 30.

[3]Lenora Tubbs Tisdale, *Preaching as Local Theology and Folk Art* (Minneapolis: Fortress Press, 1997), 57.

[4]Fred B. Craddock, *Preaching* (Nashville: Abingdon Press, 1995), 164.

[5]Frank A. Thomas, *They Like to Never Quit Praising God: The Role of Celebration in Preaching* (Cleveland: United Church Press, 1997), 5.

[6]Richard F. Ward, *Speaking from the Heart: Preaching with Passion,* Abingdon Preacher's Library (Nashville: Abingdon Press, 1992).

Chapter 7: Linda Carolyn Loving

[1]Natalie Goldberg, *Writing Down the Bones* (Boston: Shambhala, 1986), 26.

[2]Anne Lamott, *Bird by Bird* (New York: Doubleday, 1995), 28.

[3]J. Janda, *Julian* (Englewood, N.J.: Pioneer Drama Service, 1979), 29–31.

[4]Ibid., 83.

[5]Douglas Wood, *Old Turtle* (Duluth, Minn.: Pfeiffer-Hamilton, 1992).

[6]L. Montgomery, *Emily of New Moon* (New York: Bantam, 1983); Madeline L'Engle, *The Glorious Impossible* (New York: Simon & Schuster, 1990); Edwina Gately, *God Goes on Vacation* (Trabuco Canyon: Source Books, 1995); and Robert Munsch, *Love You Forever* (Ontario: Firefly Books, 1996).

[7]Madeline L'Engle, *Trailing Clouds of Glory* (Philadelphia: Westminster Press, 1985).

[8]Janda, *Julian,* 82.

[9]J. Janda, *Julian: A Play Based on the Life of Julian of Norwich* (Boston: Seabury Press, 1984), 20.

[10]*The Book of Order,* Presbyterian Church (U.S.A.), G 1.0200.

[11]Henri Nouwen, "The Vulnerable God," *Weavings* 8/4 (July/August 1993): 35.

[12]*New York Times,* 24 May 1997, section 1.

[13]Thomas Cahill, *How the Irish Saved Civilization* (New York: Anchor Books, 1995), 217.

[14]Joan Chittister, *A Passion for Life: Fragments of the Face of God* (Maryknoll, N.Y.: Orbis Books, 1996), 99.

Chapter 8: Barbara K. Lundblad

[1]Toni Morrison, *Beloved* (New York: New American Library, 1987), 88.

[2]Carol A. Newsom and Sharon H. Ringe, eds., *The Women's Bible Commentary*, rev. ed. (Louisville, Ky.: Westminster John Knox Press, 1999).

[3]Mary Oliver, *A Poetry Handbook* (New York: Harcourt Brace & Company, 1994), 122.

[4]*An Invitation to Action*, Reformed-Lutheran Dialogue Report, 1986.

[5]John Thomas, "A Mystical and Moral Presence: Unity and Renewal in the 21st Century," unpublished paper.

Chapter 9: Karen Stokes

[1]Phillips Brooks, *Lectures on Preaching* (Grand Rapids, Mich.: Baker Books, 1969), 8.

[2]Let me strongly recommend Eugene Lowry's book *The Sermon: Dancing the Edge of Mystery* (Nashville: Abingdon Press, 1997), where you will find fully elaborated these ideas, which I can barely touch upon here. This small book has been an invaluable resource for me as I seek to be intentional about what I'm up to as a preacher. In his introduction, Dr. Lowry talks about Fred Craddock's exploration of the relationship between the preacher and the congregation: "He insisted that the congregation was 'deserving [of] the right to participate' in the sermonic trip and not just be let in on the destination" (11).

[3]Eugene Lowry, class handout, August 1999, San Francisco Theological Seminary.

[4]Ibid.

[5]Eugene Lowry, *The Sermon: Dancing the Edge of Mystery* (Nashville: Abingdon Press, 1997), 23.

[6]David Steele, *The Next Voice You Hear: Sermons We Preach Together* (Louisville: Geneva Press, 1999), 29–30.

[7]Stephen Budiansky, "The Truth About Dogs," *The Atlantic Monthly*, July 1999, 39–40.

Chapter 10: Barbara Brown Taylor

[1]Reprinted with permission from *Home by Another Way* (Boston: Cowley Publications, 1999). Copyright © 1999 by Barbara Brown Taylor.

Chapter 12: Margaret Moers Wenig

[1]Eugene Lowry, *The Homiletical Plot: The Sermon as Narrative Art Form* (Atlanta: John Knox Press, 1980).

[2]This interpretation is based on Maimonides' reading as presented by Nechama Liebowitz, *Studies in Shemot, Part 1* (New York: World Zionist Congress, 1981), 149–60.

[3]*Genesis Rabbah* 55, *Sanhedrin* 89b, quoted by Rashi in his comment on Genesis 22:1.

[4]This midrash appears in a number of different versions: In one, Sarah dies upon hearing the news that Abraham has killed their son. In another, Sarah's soul departs in a sigh of joy upon hearing that Isaac is still alive. See *Tanhuma Vayera* 23, or Louis Ginzberg, *The Legends of the Jews*, trans. Henrietta Szold (New York: Jewish Publication Society of America, 1937), 1:226–87.

[5]*Genesis Rabbah* LVI:11.

[6]The title is from "Women Songs," by Kadia Molodowsky. You can find Adrienne Rich's translation of this poem in Irving Howe and Eliezer Greenberg, eds., *A Treasury of Yiddish Poetry* (New York: Holt, Rinehart & Winston, 1969), 284–85. This is not the translation I used in my sermon, but I cannot locate that translation. I am deeply grateful to

Dr. Marianne Ultmann and Gerson Goodman, members of Beth Am, The People's Temple, for listening to an earlier draft of this sermon and offering valuable criticism. I am also grateful to Rabbi Danny Zemel and the members of Temple Micah for inviting me to serve as their scholar-in-residence. I wrote this sermon for my visit to their congregation. Finally, I am grateful to my partner, Rabbi Sharon Kleinbaum, who is without question a student of Miriam.

[7]Exodus 1.1–4, 5b. All biblical quotations are from The TANAKH (JPS).

[8]Exodus 1:15–21.

[9]Exodus 2:1–9. At first Moses' mother is referred to only as "Bat Levi" (a/the daughter of Levi). Later, in verse 6:20, she is called Yochevet.

[10]Exodus 2:4, 7, 8.

[11]Exodus 2:5–10.

[12]Exodus 2:15–22, 4:18–26. Only one of Moses' sons is mentioned here by name, Gershon (2:22). Nachmanides says that Zipporah was pregnant with Eleazar when they returned to Egypt. (See note in the *Soncino Chumash,* 339.)

[13]Exodus 6:23.

[14]*Parshat Shemot* encompasses Exodus 1:1—6:1.

[15]Pharaoh's daughter certainly saved the life of a son of her "enemy." Those who believe that the midwives were Egyptians would say that they too saved lives of the sons of their enemies.

[16]At a Passover Seder, the names of the ten plagues are chanted aloud by the leader and echoed by everyone else at the table as each person removes one drop of wine from his/her cup for each plague. In preaching this sermon, I chanted the names of the plagues as they would be chanted at a Seder.

[17]*Parshat Vayera* encompasses Exodus 6:2—9:35.

[18]*Parshat Bo* encompasses Exodus 10:1—13:16.

[19]Exodus 2:4.

[20]Exodus 7:20–21.

[21]Exodus 12:1–3, 6–7, 12, 13.

[22]Genesis 18:23.

[23]Exodus 12:35.

[24]Exodus 12:36.

[25]Genesis 39:20 gives us evidence of Pharaoh's use of a prison.

[26]Moses' mother and Aaron's wife are never mentioned in a biblical story again. (Yocheved appears in another genealogy in Numbers 26:59. Elisheva's name never appears again.) Particularly noticeable is the absence of any mention of Aaron's wife at the time their two sons, Nadav and Avihu, are killed.

[27]Exodus 12:29.

[28]The ending *-ot* is, typically, the feminine plural noun ending. In the Torah and in rabbinic literature, *bechorot* is sometimes used as the plural of the masculine noun *bechor.* Given that the author had a choice, here, between *bechorot* and the more expected masculine ending *bechorim, or b'chorei mitzraim* (the [male] firstborn ones of Egypt), as in Psalm 135:8, it is good rabbinic tradition to assume that the choice of the feminine ending over the masculine ending is not arbitrary but is meant to convey some meaning.

[29]Exodus 15:1–4.

[30]Exodus 15:20–21.

[31]From Adrienne Rich, "Tattered Kaddish," *An Atlas of The Difficult World: Poems 1988–1991* (New York: Norton, 1991), 45.

[32]Even in the face of his sons' deaths, Aaron is silent/emotionless. See Leviticus 10:3.

[33]From Adrienne Rich, "Natural Resources," *The Dream of a Common Language: Poems 1974–1977* (New York: Norton, 1974), 67.

[34]The Torah gives no explanation for Nadav and Avihu's unauthorized offering of incense and strange fire (Leviticus 10:1). I am presuming that their independent spirits came from their mother and their aunt.

[35]Following the Exodus the only references to Miriam are in Numbers 12:1, 4, 5, 10, 15; 20:1(her death); 26:59; Deuteronomy 24:9; 1 Chronicles 4:17; 6:3; and Micah 6:4.

[36]From "Bridging," in Marge Piercy, *To Be of Use* (Garden City, N. Y.: Doubleday, 1973). Used with permission.

[37]Exodus 18:2.

[38]Exodus 18:7.

[39]Although Gerson and Eleazar are mentioned later in genealogies or lists of tribes, it is Joshua, not either of Moses' sons, who succeeds him.

[40]From "Women Songs" by Kadia Molodowsky.

[41]Ibid.

[42]Proverbs 31:10–31, traditionally recited at the table every Friday night by a husband to his wife.

[43]This ending occurred to me when I saw the following book title: *A Price Below Rubies: Jewish Women as Rebels and Radicals,* by Naomi Shepherd (Cambridge, Mass.: Harvard University Press, 1993).